How Airliners Fly

How Airliners Fly

a passenger's guide

Julien Evans

Airlife

Copyright © Julien Evans

1st edition published as *Is It on Autopilot?* in 1997
Reprinted 1999.

Second edition published in the UK in 2002
By Airlife Publishing Ltd

British Library Cataloguing-in-Publication Data
A catalogue record for the book
is available from the British Library

ISBN 1 84037 360 1

Photographs by Julien Evans, other than those on pages 11 and 13
courtesy Airbus Industrie, 14, 31 top, 36, 37, 38, 41, 46, 49, 56, 57
bottom, 58, 104, 106, 113 bottom, courtesy Keith Gaskell, 60, 75, 100
courtesy Detmar Härter, 117 courtesy GECAT Flight Training and
charts on pages 70, 71 supplied by Thales Avionics.

Printed in Hong Kong

*Contact us for a free catalogue that describes the complete range of
Airlife books for pilots and aviation enthusiasts.*

Airlife Publishing Ltd
101 Longden Road, Shrewsbury, SY3 9EB, England
E-mail: sales@airlifebooks.com
Website: www.airlifebooks.com

For Chris and Ali

Thanks to ...

Chris Blumenthal
Derek Gardner
Chris Joseph
Dave Lawrence
Roger May
Geoff O'Connor
John Rathbone
Roger Setchfield

Contents

Preface to the 2nd edition

In the few years since the first edition of this book was published (under its original title, 'Is It On Autopilot?') the technicalities of commercial air transport have continued to develop. On the flight decks of airliners themselves the presentation of data to pilots is now commonly by video screens rather than the separate electromechanical instruments to be found on older types. To free up airspace as traffic continues to grow, advantage has been taken of air data computer precision to standardise vertical separation between aircraft as 1,000 feet in both upper and lower airspace. Improvements in air traffic control computers and greater co-operation between adjoining nations are releasing more aircraft from the constraints of rigidly defined airways, so that more direct routings become available, easing congestion and saving time and fuel.

Likewise, modern navigational equipment has removed the necessity for directional measurement to be referenced to magnetic north and it may well be that geographic north will become the new datum, eliminating the complication of making allowance for the difference between them, which varies from place to place around the world.

Curiously, for a technical industry, aviation has still not adopted standard units when quantifying parameters. Thus distances are measured in feet, metres, kilometres and nautical miles (and in some countries, statute miles). Speeds are in knots (nautical miles per hour) or metres per second (which is how some countries report wind speed). Masses are kilograms or pounds and air pressure hectopascals (millibars) or inches of mercury. The one exception to this pot-pourri of units is that temperature is universally recorded in degrees Celsius. Perhaps in the future aviation will switch to the exclusive adoption of metric measurement, which will obviate the need for personnel in the industry to make conversions – always a possible source of human error. Speeds would be kilometres per hour and vertical distance in metres. The current standard 1,000 feet vertical separation between aircraft would change to the almost identical 300 metres.

As commercial air transport moves into its second century, its future is overshadowed by two uncertainties – its vulnerability to terrorist attack and its impact on the environment. The solutions to these problems are primarily the responsibility of the world's political leaders, although technologists will play their part. Today's jetliners are very much more fuel-efficient than their predecessors and when their seats are filled they can match other methods of people transportation in minimising environmental damage to our delicate planet. But it may well be that kerosene – cheap and easily produced – will one day become unacceptable as the main propellant for airliners. There are alternatives, which are mentioned in the final chapter of this book, but the travelling public may have to meet the cost of their implementation.

Let us hope that the difficulties can be resolved, so that future generations of pilots and passengers may continue to enjoy the privilege of flight.

Introduction

Millions of people travel by air every day. For many of them their only concern is that they depart on time, that the flight is comfortable and that they arrive safely. They will not bother themselves about the technicalities of flight and will take speed and convenience for granted. And why shouldn't they? Commercial air travel is now a mature industry and passengers' expectations are high.

But for many people aviation is something more than mere transportation. They find fascination and delight in the flight of aircraft of all sorts. They marvel that a machine weighing perhaps 400 tonnes can lift itself into the air and propel itself through the heavens at speeds over 500 miles per hour. If they are sitting inside one of them their curiosity might lead them to ask for permission to visit the flight deck and if they are lucky – and regulations permit – they will be allowed to do so.

What will the flight deck visitor see? Two, or possibly three people, apparently doing very little, surrounded by a bewildering array of display screens, switches and controls. The aircraft will look as if it is flying itself. Certainly no one will seem to be holding the 'steering wheels'. If the ground is visible the visitor will perhaps remark that the aircraft appears to be hardly moving. The pilots will explain that the sensation of speed is absent because there is nothing nearby to judge it against, with the aircraft cruising several miles above the earth's surface. In cloud, or over the sea, or at night, the visitor might naturally ask how the pilots know where they are going. The answer, of course, is that they are not concerned if nothing is visible outside because all the information they need is displayed on the panels in front of them.

The visitor might have other questions. How high are we? How fast are we going? How do you remember what all the switches do? What happens if the engines stop? How long does it take to train as a pilot? How much fuel does it need? What happens if we fly into a storm?

This book is intended to answer questions such as these in language that can be easily understood. Of course, aviation is a highly technical subject, but most people will find that they can grasp the basics without too much difficulty. Although enthusiasts wonder at the capabilities of flying machines, ranging from hang gliders to supersonic fighters to large airliners, the truth is that there is nothing mysterious about them. It is not magic that keeps them aloft, but the laws of science.

In keeping with its technical background the language of aviation is peppered with acronyms and abbreviations, not for effect but to ease communication between persons occupied in the industry. In this book I have minimised the use of acronyms where possible and, where they do crop up, I have repeated their full nomenclature from time to time as a reminder. For convenience there is also a glossary. Occasionally, for the sake of clarity, I have oversimplified some technical aspects and taken minor liberties with scientific accuracy. I hope readers disciplined in these subjects will not be offended.

Where specific data pertaining to the Boeing 767 is included in the text, it relates to the model 767-300 version of this aircraft, powered by General Electric CF6 80C2 engines.

In this book the word 'pilot' includes both captains and copilots, whose separate roles will come to light as the text progresses. Given its subject matter, it is understandable that pilots are mentioned more frequently than other personnel in the industry, but they will be the first to admit that no airliner would ever get off the ground without the contribution of the others. Many of them are directly involved with the operation of aircraft, such as cabin crew, engineers and air traffic controllers. Many more have indirect roles to play, including managers, operations staff and ground handling agents. It must be acknowledged that their efforts are no less important than those of the men and women sitting in the pilots' seats in the flight deck.

On the tricky subject of personal pronouns I have used the currently favoured 'he or she' and 'him or her' constructions except where repeated use makes the text clumsy, whereupon I have reverted to 'he' and 'him', asking the reader to assume the inclusion of the feminine forms by inference. Again I hope this *modus scribendi* is acceptable to female readers.

Finally, it has to be said that pilots will disagree with the comment above that there is nothing magical about aviation. After all, it was the magic of flight that led them to a career in the skies. And perhaps some readers of this book might themselves feel the same spark and turn their thoughts in the same direction. Who knows, perhaps one day they might find themselves sitting at the controls of a jet airliner, listening to a flight deck visitor asking: 'Is it on autopilot?'

1
The Hardware

The airframe

The modern airliner is constructed mainly from aluminium alloy, which is both strong and light. Nowadays some parts of the structure might be made of non-metallic materials, such as carbon fibre composite, which is as strong as aluminium alloy but even lighter. Without its engines, the remainder of the aircraft is referred to as the **airframe**.

The overall shape of the airliner is determined by aerodynamic factors. Aerodynamics is the study of the behaviour of objects as they pass through the air. What do we need to transport a useful load through the skies? Obviously, the first requirement is a container to hold the load. This container is the called the **fuselage** and generally takes the form of a cylindrical structure. The front end is its **nose** and the rear end is its **tail**.

How do we lift the fuselage and its load into the air? This is the purpose of the **wings**, which generate the lifting force when air flows past them. At the tail of the fuselage are attached the **fin** and **tailplane**. This

A view across today's modern modular A320 Airbus assembly line at Toulouse. Each aircraft is brought to final assembly stage on the line, with engines in place, before being moved to a separate bay to receive its final equipment.

assembly strongly resembles the arrangement of tail feathers to be found on arrows and darts. Indeed, it serves the same function, which is to keep the fuselage pointing in the direction of flight. In American parlance the fin is the **vertical stabilizer** and the tailplane the **horizontal stabilizer**.

Parts of the structure are moveable, rather than rigidly fixed. Along the front edge of each wing, the **leading edge**, are moveable sections called **slats**. Along the rear edge, the **trailing edge**, are **flaps** and **ailerons**. On the top surfaces of the wings, just ahead of the flaps, are **spoilers**. The moveable part of the fin is the **rudder**. The left and right sections of the tailplane feature moveable parts called **elevators**. All these moveable parts are collectively termed the **flight controls**. They have their effect by changing the airflow patterns around the aircraft and, as the name suggests, they enable the pilot to control the flight path of the aircraft.

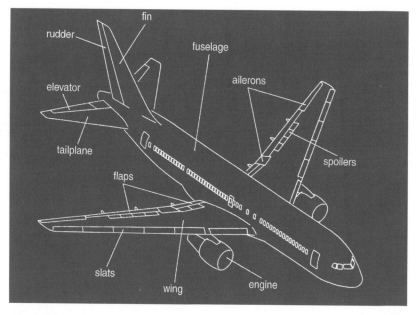

Fig. 1. The airliner.

We need something to support the aircraft when it is on the ground and this is the purpose of the **landing gear** (or **undercarriage**). In the **tricycle** arrangement, which is the most common, there are two **mainwheel** units and one **nosewheel** unit. Each mainwheel unit is located where the wing joins the fuselage and comprises an assembly of two or four wheels. The mainwheels are fitted with anti-skid brakes. The nosewheel unit is to be found where its name suggests and will typically have two wheels. Nearly the whole mass of the aircraft is borne by the mainwheels. Very large airliners have additional landing gear units. For example, the Airbus A340 has one extra mainwheel unit between the other two and the Boeing 747 has two extra units. These additional wheels spread the load taken by the runways and taxiways on which the aircraft manoeuvre.

The landing gear units are retractable, meaning that they can be folded up into the body of the aircraft once it is airborne. The landing gear is normally retracted immediately after take-off and is extended again during the approach to landing.

For greater conspicuity to other traffic, airliners carry red and white flashing lights on their fuselages and wing tips. Powerful **landing lights** are mounted on the wings and landing gear for illumination of runways and taxiways at night. To comply with night flying regulations aircraft must also carry other external lights. These are a red light at the left wing tip, a green light at the right, and rearward facing white lights.

This is the prototype A319, seen in June 1995, having been fitted with its fin and tailplane assembly at Hamburg. Its painted fin leaves no doubt as to the provenance of the new type. This aircraft made its maiden flight in August 1995, ahead of schedule.

The engines

As anyone who has held his or her hand out of the window of a fast-moving car can testify, the air tries to resist the motion of objects passing through it. In aerodynamics, the resistance is called **drag**. This is why the landing gear is retracted after take-off, so that its drag is removed. The aircraft needs a method of propulsion to overcome the remaining drag and keep pushing it through the air so that the wings continue to generate lift. The propulsive force is provided by the engines. So how does a glider stay aloft if it has no engines? And more to the point, can an airliner continue to fly if all its engines have stopped? We'll go into this matter later. For the moment, you'll be delighted to hear that the answer to the latter question is, in general terms, 'yes'.

Large modern airliners are powered by jet engines. The basic principle is that ambient air is drawn into the front of the engine and compressed by a large fan. The fan, which is encased in a cowling, forces the compressed air backwards in the form of a jet, much in the manner of a domestic electric fan. The engine itself experiences an equal and

The fan is mounted at the forward end of the low pressure spool.

The cowling is easily opened for access to the engine's inner parts when maintenance is required.

opposite force and this is the forward-acting thrust which propels the aircraft. Some of the compressed air flows into the combustion chamber, where fuel is injected into it and ignited. Combustion of the fuel generates heat which increases the air pressure even further. This highly compressed air now escapes from the rear of the engine, joining the air driven back from the compressor fan and adding to the total engine thrust.

A more detailed examination of a typical jet engine shows that after the hot, compressed air leaves the combustion chamber it drives a turbine before it escapes. This turbine, which is another fan-like array of blades, is mounted on an axle, or spool, on which is fixed the compressor fan at the front of the engine. Once the engine is running, then, the turbine is driving the fan.

Expanding a little further, we can see that there are usually two compressors and two turbines in the engine. From front to rear the sequence of components is: low-pressure compressor (which includes the fan), high-pressure compressor, high-pressure turbine and low-pressure turbine. The low-pressure compressor is driven by the low-pressure turbine

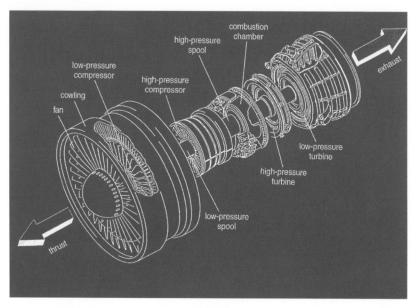

Fig. 2. The jet engine.

on one spool. The high-pressure compressor is driven by the high-pressure turbine. These two components are mounted on their own spool, which is hollow and runs concentrically outside the low-pressure spool.

Another feature of the engine is its **reverser**. When activated, reverser doors in the cowling block the rearward flow of the fan air and direct the thrust outwards and forwards. The reversers are used during landing to assist in slowing the aircraft down after touchdown.

The engine starter is a separate small turbine. When activated, compressed air from an external source spins the starter, which is connected by gear wheels to the high-pressure spool. Rotation of this spool induces a flow of air through the engine, which in turn causes the low-pressure spool to rotate. When the high-pressure spool has attained its start-up speed of rotation, fuel is introduced to the combustion chamber and ignited by a spark plug, similar to those in car engines. Once both spools have accelerated to their self-sustaining idling speeds the starter is disconnected and the ignitor switched off. Now the fuel entering the combustion chamber is ignited by that already burning. After flight the engines are stopped simply by shutting off their fuel supplies.

Most airliners are powered by two engines, usually mounted on pylons under the leading edge of each wing near the fuselage. Another common location for the engines is either side of the rear fuselage near the tail. Some large airliners have three or four engines.

The fan produces the greater part of the total engine thrust.

Besides their chief task of propelling the aircraft, the engines also supply power for the aircraft's various systems, as we shall see later. The fuel for jet engines is kerosene, a less volatile liquid than petrol, similar in its characteristics to domestic paraffin. It is stored in tanks in the wing structure and fuselage and supplied to the engines by fuel pumps. The combustion products are mainly carbon dioxide and water vapour. In the cold upper atmosphere the water vapour instantly freezes into ice crystals, visible as the white **contrails** (condensation trails) streaming from the aircraft's engines.

The electrical system

Each engine drives an electrical generator, very similar in function to the alternator found in car engines. Additionally the aircraft will be equipped with an **auxiliary power unit (APU)**. The APU is a small gas turbine engine, similar in operation to the jet engine, usually mounted in the tail, which drives its own separate generator. In normal operation the engine generators share the load of powering the various aircraft systems which require electrical power and the APU is switched off.

In the event of failure of one of the engine generators, the APU can be started and its generator used to replace the failed generator. If a second generator fails, the aircraft's electrical system will reconfigure itself

Individual circuit breakers (CBs) protect the electrical services.

so that non-essential electrical services are isolated from the system and all essential services are supplied by the remaining functioning generator. If all generators fail, further load-shedding takes place and the aircraft's batteries supply vital electrical services.

Every electrical service in the aircraft is protected by a **circuit breaker (CB)**. Any fault which allows excessive electric current to be supplied is detected by the CB, which pops out or **trips**, much like a domestic CB. Tripping isolates the faulty service and prevents electrical overheating.

The hydraulic system

On small aircraft, the pilot can move the flight controls directly by inputs from the control wheel, which is mechanically linked to them. It is not difficult to move the controls against the restoring force of the airflow because the control surfaces are not big.

The flight control surfaces on an airliner are far too big to be moved by human muscle alone. Instead, the pilot's control wheel inputs are sent to **actuators** attached to each flight control. These inputs adjust valves in the actuator which controls the flow of pressurised hydraulic fluid through it. Thus it is hydraulic pressure which actually moves the flight controls. The control wheel inputs are sent to the actuator valves either mechanically (with cables or rods) or, in some more recent designs, electrically. This latter is the so-called fly-by-wire system.

As with the aircraft's electrical system, extensive provision is made for back-ups in the event of hydraulic system failures. Typically, the airliner will have three hydraulic systems, each independent of the other two. The primary flight controls, in other words the elevators, ailerons and rudder, each have three actuators, one supplied by each hydraulic system. Thus even with two systems failed the pilot still has full control of the aircraft.

Besides the flight controls (including the slats, flaps and spoilers), the hydraulic systems also power the landing gear extension and retraction mechanisms (which account for some of the mechanical noises heard in the cabin during take-off and landing), the nosewheel steering mechanism (for steering the aircraft on the ground) and the wheel brakes. On some airliners they also extend and retract the engine thrust reversers doors.

The fluid used in aircraft hydraulic systems is a specially-formulated oil. The three systems each have their own reservoir of fluid, from which the fluid is pumped under pressure to the user components. The pumps are powered from several sources, including the main engines themselves and the electrical system. Splitting the power sources in this manner enables a hydraulic system to remain operational even if one of its pumps fails.

The pneumatic system

Another function of the main engines is to supply compressed air to the cabin in the fuselage. Jet airliners cruise at heights in the region of 30,000 to 45,000 feet, where the ambient air is far too thin and too cold to support normal breathing. By pressurising the cabin with warm, compressed air from the engines, a more normal environment is achieved. Typically, the air in the cabin will simulate a real height of about 6,000 feet above sea level, at which normal breathing is possible.

Allied to the pressurisation system are the air conditioning packs. In fact the air supplied from the engines passes through the packs, which control its temperature, before entering the cabin. On the ground, with the engines switched off, the auxiliary power unit supplies air to the packs, so that even in hot climates the environment in the cabin can be maintained at a comfortable temperature. This source of air is also used to drive the main engine starters, as described previously.

As with the other aircraft systems we have looked at, the pressurisation system features back-up arrangements in case of failures. For example, the remaining air conditioning packs are capable of pressurising the cabin to a normal level if one of them fails. However, if the cabin does lose its air pressure for any reason then a supply of oxygen is provided for every passenger and crew member through individual face-masks. These masks drop down from their stowage automatically if the pressure falls below a predetermined level.

Warm air from the engines also supplies the anti-icing system. When the aircraft is flying in cloud in freezing conditions, any ice build-up on the engines and wings is melted by this air, which is directed along special ducts designed for this purpose.

2
The Flight Deck

The flight deck has seats for two pilots (and in some older designs a flight engineer seated behind them). It is usual for the captain to take the left seat and the copilot the right seat. Arrayed around the pilots' seats are controls for the aircraft and its systems and display panels and indicators (or **instruments**) to tell the pilots how the aircraft and its systems are behaving.

The flight controls

In front of each pilot is a **control wheel**, which looks like the lower part of a car's steering wheel mounted on a column. The wheel can be turned left and right and also pulled back and pushed forward on its column. The left and right inputs are connected to hydraulic actuators in the aircraft's ailerons and spoilers. The pulling and pushing inputs are connected to actuators in the elevators. The two control wheels are interlinked so that they both move together regardless of which pilot is making the input.

On the later designs of airliner built by Airbus a **side stick** replaces the control wheel, one mounted to the left of the left-hand seat pilot, the other to the right of the right-hand seat pilot. Moving the stick sideways has the same effect as turning the control wheel described above. Forward and backward movement of the side stick likewise has the same effect as pushing or pulling the control wheel.

At the feet of each pilot are two **rudder pedals**, one for each foot. When the left pedal is pushed forward the right pedal moves back, and vice versa. The pedal inputs are connected to actuators in the rudder. As with the control wheels, the two sets of pedals are interlinked.

Between the pilots' seats is the **console**, on which are located several controls. One of these is the **flap lever**. This lever is mounted on a quadrant and can be moved to various detents on the quadrant. Its movement is connected to actuators in the flaps and slats. If the normal flap and slat operating system fails a back-up system is available.

On each pilot's control wheel is a switch which can be pressed up or down with the thumb. The input from these **stabilizer trim** switches is connected to actuators in the tail of the aircraft which change the angle at which the tailplane is set. If the normal control is inoperative a back-up control is available, mounted on the console.

Also on the console is to be found the **speedbrake lever**, mounted on a quadrant like the flap lever, but without discrete detented positions. Its movement is connected to actuators in the spoilers.

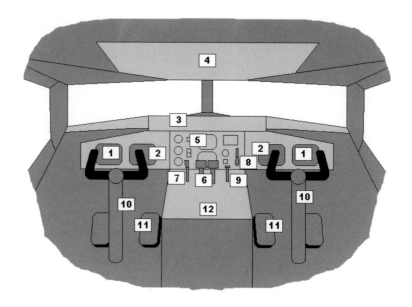

1	Primary Flight Display
2	Navigation Display
3	Glareshield
4	Overhead Panel
5	Instrument Panel
6	Thrust Levers
7	Speedbrake Lever
8	Landing Gear Lever
9	Flap Lever
10	Control Wheel
11	Rudder Pedals
12	Console

Fig. 3. The flight deck.

The **instrument panel** extends across the flight deck in front of the pilots. On the centre instrument panel will be found the **landing gear lever**. Raising this lever retracts the landing gear. Lowering the lever extends the gear.

Engine controls

The main engine thrust is controlled by levers located at the forward end of the console. Each engine has its own **thrust lever** (or throttle). Unlike the accelerator pedal in a car, the thrust levers are not spring-loaded to

Boeing 757 centre instrument panel (above) and console (below). In the foreground are controls for the communications and navigation radios.

the idle thrust position. Instead they retain the position in which they are set. The reverser controls are attached to the thrust levers.

Just behind the thrust levers are to be found the **fuel control switches**, which control the valves admitting fuel to the engines. The fuel supply is opened during the engine start sequence and closed to shut down the engines when they are no longer required.

The instrument panel

On newer airliners, there are two main displays in front of each pilot. One shows **primary flight** parameters and the other **navigational** data.

The centre indicator in the flight display is the attitude indicator (AI). Its appearance is a pictorial representation of the view outside. The symbol in the middle of the AI is the attitude datum and it represents the aircraft itself. Behind this datum is shown the earth's horizon. By looking at the AI, then, the pilot can see the aircraft's **attitude**, in other words whether the aircraft's nose is pointing above or below the horizon and also whether the wings are tilted to the left or right. The AI is therefore of vital importance when flying in cloud, or at night, when

Fig. 4. The attitude indicator.

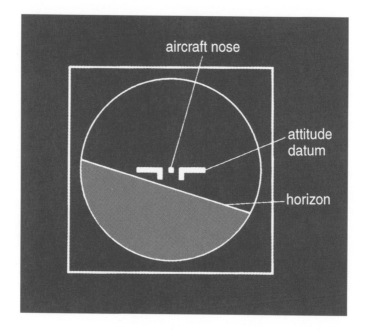

the earth's natural horizon cannot be seen. In the example shown the nose is above the horizon and the wings are tilted to the left.

To the left of the AI is the **airspeed indicator** (ASI). As its name suggests it tells the pilots the speed of the aircraft through the air. As we shall see later, this may differ considerably from its speed over the ground. The ASI is calibrated in **knots**, which are nautical miles per hour. To the right of the AI is the **altimeter**, which shows the aircraft's altitude or height. It is calibrated in **feet**. (In the world of aviation, the words 'altitude' and 'height' have different definitions. We'll meet them again later in the book, but at the moment the difference need not concern us.) Also to be found on the flight display is the **vertical speed indicator (VSI)**. As its name suggests, it tells the pilots how quickly the aircraft is climbing or descending. It is calibrated in **feet per minute**.

The main feature on the navigational display is the **horizontal situation indicator (HSI)**. The HSI is usually in the form of a map display, showing the aircraft's geographic position in relation to the planned route. It also indicates the aircraft's **heading**, in other words the direction the nose is pointing in relative to north. Additionally there are pointers showing the direction in which nearby radio beacons are located.

On older aircraft types, flight and navigational data is presented on discrete electromechanical instruments. In case of failure of the

Copilot's instrument panel on the 757, a mix of data screens and electromechanical instruments.

primary displays or instruments there will also be a set of standby instruments mounted on the centre instrument panel. They will include an AI, an ASI and an altimeter.

The engine instruments

Also on the centre instrument panel are the engine instruments. Amongst other things, they tell the pilots:

- the level of thrust the engines are developing
- the speed of rotation of the high-pressure and low-pressure spools
- the rate of fuel consumption
- the temperature of the exhaust gases

Boeing 757-200 centre instrument panel. The centre screens indicate engine data and systems status.

Radio controls

Communication between the pilots and air traffic control (ATC) is usually by very high frequency (VHF) radio. In some parts of the world where VHF coverage is not available (for example over the oceans and sparsely populated areas) communication with ATC is by high frequency (HF) radio. HF has the advantage of considerably greater range than VHF but the disadvantage of much higher background noise and interference. With the steady expansion of satellite-based voice communication it is likely that use of HF radio will gradually be phased out.

The pilots each wear a headset, comprising two earphones and a microphone mounted on a boom. To transmit a message to ATC they press a transmitter button and speak into the microphone. Messages from ATC are received in the earphones. The aircraft will also have an interphone system, which connects the pilots' headsets to telephone-type handsets in the cabin, enabling them to communicate with the cabin crew.

The controls for the aircraft's radio equipment are usually to be found on the console. They include knobs which are turned to change the transmitter and receiver frequencies. Some of the radio equipment is for navigation rather than communication purposes. We shall examine this in greater detail later on.

The overhead panel

In the flight deck ceiling is located the overhead panel. On it are mounted controls and indicators for the various aircraft systems. They include:

- the electrical system
- the hydraulic system
- the pneumatic system
- the fuel system
- the anti-icing system
- the engine starter controls

Controls for most of the aircraft's systems are located in the overhead panel.

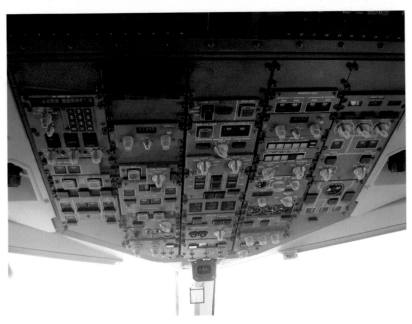

The glareshield

Besides shielding the instrument panel from direct sunlight, the glareshield also houses controls for the aircraft's autopilot.

The 757 glareshield.

3
How Does It Fly?

It is surely a thrilling sight to watch a large modern airliner accelerate along a runway, gently raise its nose and smoothly lift itself into the air. In the case of the Boeing 747 we are talking in terms of almost 400 tonnes (400,000 kilograms). How can something as insubstantial as air support this sort of mass?

The answer lies in the shape of the wing. As it moves through the air the curved wing shape speeds up the flow over the upper surface, which causes the air to lose some of its natural pressure, since the laws of physics demand that the sum total of its energy (that is, its energy of movement and its pressure energy) must remain constant. In other words, wing motion through the air creates a partial vacuum above it. The air at normal pressure underneath the wing therefore exerts a push force upwards and this is the **lift** force that keeps the aircraft flying.

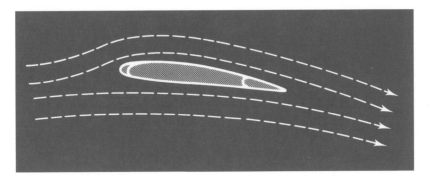

Fig. 5. Airflow past wing.

How much lift can a wing generate? There are several factors which determine the lifting ability of a wing. Firstly, its shape. From what was stated above we would expect that the more highly curved the shape was, the more lift would be generated, and this conclusion is indeed borne out in practice. But there is a drawback, and that is that a highly curved wing shape also generates greater **drag**, (the air resistance to the forward motion of the wing). A less curved, more streamlined wing shape will produce less drag – but also less lift. How do we solve the dilemma?

In the case of the jet airliner the prime requirement is high cruising speed. The lower the drag generated by the aircraft and its wings, the greater will be the speed at which the engines can propel it through the air. This brings us to the second factor controlling lift, which is speed. The faster the wings move through the air the more lift they produce. And now we can see why the wing shape of the jet airliner is highly streamlined rather than greatly curved. At high speed these wings will generate enough lift to support the mass of the aircraft.

But what about take-off and landing? The aircraft needs to be able to fly at much lower speeds, otherwise runways would have to be ridiculously long. Lower take-off and landing speeds also reduce the stresses on the landing gear and tyres.

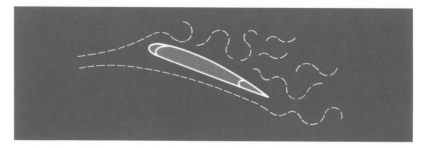

Fig. 6. Stalled wing.

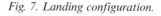

One way to increase lift at low speed is to increase the **angle of attack** of the wing. This is the angle at which it meets the airflow. As you would expect, the greater the angle of attack, the more lift is generated. But there is a snag here – if the angle is increased too much, the smooth airflow pattern past the wing breaks up into turbulent eddies. When this happens the wing is said to have **stalled**. A stalled wing generates only a fraction of its normal lift. An aircraft with stalled wings will lose height rapidly and its pilot will experience loss of control to a lesser or greater degree.

Fig. 7. Landing configuration.

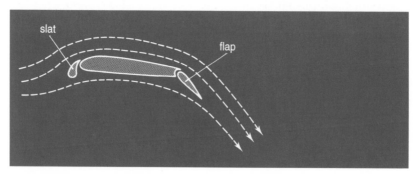

The landing and take-off problem is solved by the use of flaps and slats. Remember that these are moveable parts of the wing attached to the trailing and leading edges. In cruising flight the flaps and slats are retracted, giving the wings their most streamlined shape. For take-off, they are partly extended to accentuate the wing curve in order to increase lift without too great a drag penalty. For landing, the flaps and slats are fully extended to generate maximum lift. The associated extra drag is now beneficial in minimising the runway length required.

The winglets at the tips of the MD-11 wings reduce aerodynamic drag.

On this 737 the slats and flaps are fully extended for landing.

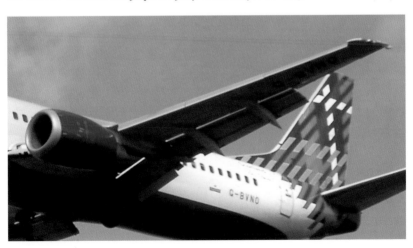

4
How Do We Fly It?

The most obvious difference between aircraft and ground-based vehicles is the freedom of the former to move in the third dimension. The pilot must be able to control the **vertical** (up-and-down) path of the aircraft as well as its **horizontal** (left-and-right) path and the **speed** at which it is flying. The former two are controlled by inputs from the control wheel. Speed is controlled by either control wheel inputs or engine thrust setting. Straightaway we can point out a fundamental difference between nautical and aeronautical navigation. The **heading** of a waterborne craft (in other words the direction it is pointing) is controlled by the craft's rudder. *The rudder of an aircraft, by contrast, is not used to control heading during flight.*

The primary flight controls

The primary flight controls are the ailerons, elevators and rudder. As we have already seen, the ailerons and elevators are connected to the control wheel and the rudder to the rudder pedals. The control wheel can be turned from side to side (like a car's steering wheel). Additionally it can be pulled towards the pilot or pushed away from him or her. When it is turned to the left, the ailerons on the left wing move up and those on the right wing move down. If the wheel movement is large, the spoilers on the left wing also move up. If the wheel is moved to the right the ailerons move in the opposite sense and the spoilers on the right wing move up.

Fig. 8. Aileron and spoiler movement. The control wheel has been turned to the left.

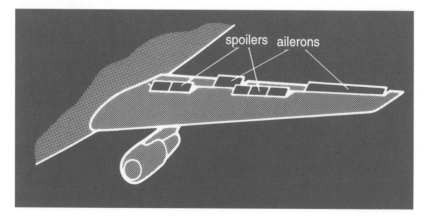

The effect of the aileron and spoiler movement is to change the airflow patterns over the wings. If the left ailerons are up, the curvature of the upper wing surface is reduced, in turn reducing the lift generated. Additionally the raised spoilers will partially disrupt the airflow, further reducing lift. Conversely, the lowered ailerons on the right wing will increase the wing curvature and so increase the lift generated by the right wing. In other words, if the pilot moves the wheel to the left the left wing will go down and the right wing up. This motion is called **rolling to the left**. Moving the wheel to the right makes the aircraft roll to the right.

When the control wheel is pulled back, the elevators move upwards, and vice versa. The elevator position determines the airflow pattern past the tailplane. Raised elevators deflect the airflow upwards, which means that the tailplane experiences a downward force. Of course the opposite is also true. Therefore, if the pilot pulls the wheel back the aircraft will raise its nose. If he or she pushes it forwards the aircraft's nose will drop. This motion is called **pitching**.

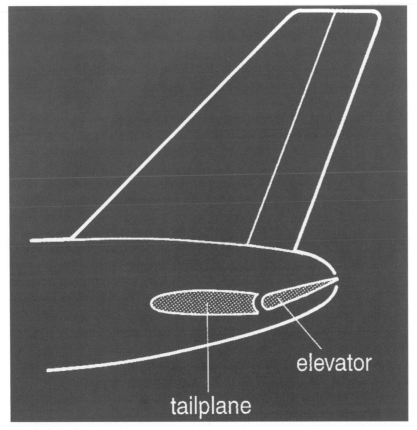

Fig. 9. Raised elevators.

When the left rudder pedal is pushed forward the rudder moves to the left, and vice versa. The rudder position determines the airflow pattern past the fin, which consequently affects the force experienced by the fin. For example, if the pilot pushes the left pedal forward, the nose of the aircraft moves to the left (because the tail moves to the right). If he or she pushes the right pedal forward then the nose movement will be to the right. This motion is called **yawing**. So why can't we turn the aircraft using the rudder pedals? The answer is that we can, but we don't. We'll see why later.

Thrust control

If the pilot pushes the thrust levers (or throttles) forward, the fuel flow to the combustion chambers in the engines is increased and the engines develop greater thrust. Retarding the levers reduces engine thrust. To select reverse thrust, the forward thrust levers are retarded to idle and the reverse thrust levers are pulled upwards. To increase reverse thrust, these levers are pulled further upwards. On most designs of airliner, selection of reverse thrust is mechanically inhibited in flight.

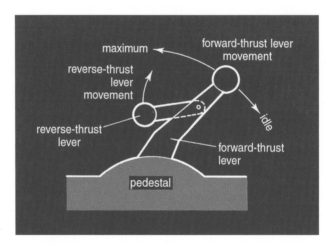

Fig. 10. Thrust lever.

Pitch attitude and pitch control

The pitch attitude relates to the aircraft's nose position in the vertical sense. The pilot assesses the aircraft's pitch attitude by reference to the attitude indicator (AI). Pulling the control wheel back raises the nose to a higher pitch attitude. Pushing it forwards lowers the nose to a lower pitch attitude. Of course, these pitching motions change the angle of attack of the wings and therefore affect the wing lift.

Bank attitude and roll control

The bank attitude relates to the lateral position of the wings. If the wings are not level, they are said to be in a banked attitude. Again, the pilot assesses the aircraft's bank by reference to the AI. As we have seen, turning the control wheel left lowers the left wing and raises the right wing, and vice versa. The rolling motion continues until the wheel is centred. *When the wheel is centred the aircraft will maintain the bank attitude it happens to be in.*

Speed control

The second factor affecting the aircraft's flight path is its **airspeed**. The pilot can control speed by two methods. One is to change the thrust setting of the engines. For example, increasing the engine thrust in level flight (not climbing or descending) makes the aircraft accelerate, and vice versa. The second method of controlling speed is by change of pitch attitude. If the thrust setting is fixed, lowering the nose with the control wheel will make the aircraft accelerate. Raising the nose will make it decelerate. The method chosen depends on the phase of flight.

Vertical flight path and speed

The combination of pitch attitude setting and thrust setting will determine whether the aircraft flies level or climbs or descends, and also the speed at which it flies. To make the aircraft achieve a desired vertical flight path and speed the pilot must select the appropriate pitch attitude and thrust setting. Only one combination will give the correct result. Expanding what was said above about phases of flight, the pitch attitude chosen by the pilot is sometimes used to control the vertical flight path of the aircraft and sometimes to control its speed.

Level flight

In level flight the aircraft neither gains nor loses altitude. In other words the indication on the **altimeter** remains constant. In level flight the vertical flight path is controlled by pitch attitude and the speed is controlled by thrust setting. If an undesired increase in altitude is observed, the pilot will move the control wheel slightly forward to set a lower pitch attitude and thus correct the error. If the speed is too high, the pilot will retard the thrust levers slightly. An increase of thrust will be necessary if the speed is too low.

Climbing flight

In climbing flight the engines are set to climb thrust. The aircraft's speed is therefore controlled by pitch attitude. If the indicated speed is too low, the pilot will move the control wheel forward to set a lower pitch attitude. If the speed is too high, a higher attitude will be needed.

In climbing flight the aircraft's speed is controlled by pitch attitude (Cathay Pacific A340).

Descending flight

The controls are used as for the climb. In other words the speed is controlled by pitch attitude and the rate of descent is controlled by thrust setting. At its normal descent speed and with its engines at idle thrust the typical jet airliner will glide at an angle of about 1:20. If engine thrust is increased the aircraft will begin to accelerate and so to maintain normal speed a higher nose attitude will be needed. This new combination of pitch attitude and thrust setting will result in a reduced rate of descent and hence a shallower descent gradient. (If the process is repeated sufficiently you can see that the aircraft will eventually attain a level flight path and further repetition will result in a climb.) When approaching to land, however, the controls are used differently. Now the pitch attitude is adjusted as necessary to control the vertical flight path, in this case to achieve the correct approach angle, while thrust is set as necessary to control speed.

Turning

When the wings are level the aircraft will fly straight and the horizontal situation indicator (HSI) will show a constant heading. The HSI is referenced to **magnetic north**, which is the datum for navigation.

747 on final approach, speed controlled by engine thrust and vertical path by the elevators.

To start a turn, the control wheel is turned in the desired direction until the desired bank attitude is attained. Then the wheel is centred again. The bank will remain at the attained attitude and the tilted lift force will make the aircraft turn, with the HSI showing a changing heading. Note the difference between turning a car and turning an aircraft. In a car the steering wheel must be held in its displaced position to maintain the turn, whereas *the aircraft will turn whenever the wings are banked, even though the control wheel is centred.* Therefore to stop the turn the control wheel must be turned away from the lower wing to level the wings again. If the wings are level the aircraft will fly straight. If they are not, the aircraft will turn towards the lower wing. The greater the angle of bank, the more quickly the aircraft will turn. Of course, this is true regardless of whether it is climbing, descending or flying level.

Fig. 11. The banked turn.

The rudder is the moveable part of the fin.

What is the rudder for?

Why do we bank the wings to turn the aircraft? Why don't we use the rudder? The answer is that the turn has to be **balanced**. If we used the rudder to turn, the aircraft would **skid** and its passengers would be flung to one side, much as they would in a car which takes a corner at high speed. If however we bank the wings to turn, the outward force is balanced by the tilted attitude and so the occupants of the aircraft feel no sideways force one way or the other. Watch what happens to your cup of coffee (or glass of wine) the next time you fly. You will notice that the liquid surface lies parallel to the rim of the cup (or glass) even when the aircraft is in a banked turn. Aerodynamically, this technique is the best to follow because the airflow past the aircraft is symmetrical and therefore no extra drag is incurred.

Why do we need a rudder at all, then? Well, there are times when we can't control heading with wing bank, for example during take-off and landing. Keeping straight on the runway will require inputs from the rudder. As we shall see later, there may also be occasions in flight where use of the rudder is necessary.

Stall avoidance

Earlier on we saw that attempting to fly with the wings at too high an angle of attack made the airflow pattern break up and that this caused the wing to stall. A stalled aircraft loses height rapidly and brings control problems for the pilot. Clearly the stall is something to be avoided at all costs.

How does the pilot know if the wings are close to the stalling angle? One solution would be an angle of attack indicator and indeed some aircraft are fitted with just such an instrument. Otherwise the best clue is the indicated airspeed. Why? Because of the relationship between angle of attack and airspeed. Remember that at high speed only a shallow angle of attack is needed to generate enough lift to support the aircraft. But at lower speeds, higher angles are needed. In other words, *the lower the indicated airspeed, the higher is the angle of attack of the wings.* If the pilot allows the airspeed to keep falling, the wings will reach the stalling angle and the aircraft will stall. The speed at which this happens is called the **stalling speed**.

If the aircraft is heavily loaded then in order to generate the extra lift required it needs to fly faster at any given angle of attack than if it was lightly loaded. This relationship still holds true as the stalling angle is approached. In other words, the more heavily the aircraft is loaded, the greater will be its stalling speed.

But what about the flaps and slats? Don't they allow flight at lower speeds for take-off and landing? The answer is: yes, they do, because they increase lift at lower speeds *without increasing the angle of attack.* Of course, even with the flaps and slats fully extended, progressive reduction of airspeed will eventually bring about a stall.

For every aircraft type, an assessment is made of its stalling characteristics before it enters service. Included in the **Flight Manual**, which is the book of instructions, will be information about the minimum safe airspeeds that can be accepted for any combination of aircraft mass and flap setting. (From now on, the phrase 'flap setting' means by implication 'flap-and-slat setting'.)

For the pilot, then, stall avoidance is achieved by ensuring that the indicated airspeed is not allowed to fall below the minimum safe value for the flap setting in use. If by some mischance the speed drops too low, angle of attack sensors will activate a warning system. This consists of a device which makes the control wheel column shake rapidly. A pilot sensing activation of the 'stick shaker' will take immediate corrective action, which is to increase engine thrust to maximum (thrust levers fully forward) and to move the control wheel forward to pitch the aircraft nose down to an attitude at which it can accelerate away from the stalling speed.

Flaps and slats

The extension and retraction of the flaps and slats are controlled by the flap lever. Typically there will be several detents on the quadrant, allowing the lever to select particular settings. The flap lever controls both the flaps and slats.

Sri Lankan A340 in landing configuration. Note supplementary main landing gear unit under the fuselage.

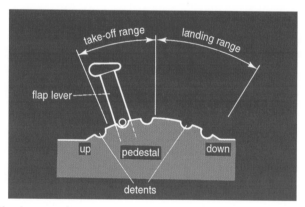

Fig. 12. Flap lever quadrant.

In the take-off range the flaps are partially extended. The more the lever is moved away from the UP position the more the flaps are extended. Movement of the lever into the landing range makes the flaps extend further. Slat extension is simpler. Usually there are only three degrees of deployment: up (fully retracted), take-off (partially extended – flap lever in take-off range) and landing (fully extended – lever in landing range). A gauge on the centre instrument panel shows the pilots the position attained by the flaps.

For take-off, the flap lever is positioned to one of the take-off detents. Which one should we choose? That depends on several factors, the main one being the length of runway available. We shall look at this subject in a bit more detail when we consider aircraft performance. Once we have achieved a safe height after getting airborne, we lower the nose to make the aircraft accelerate. As the speed increases so the flap lever can be moved through the detents to the up position.

For the approach to landing the opposite process occurs. As the aircraft slows down the flaps are extended to progressively greater settings. For the landing itself they are selected fully down.

Spoilers

The spoilers are hinged panels located just ahead of the flaps. When the speedbrake lever is pulled back the spoilers hinge upwards, greater lever movement causing greater spoiler deployment. Their function, as their name suggests, is to spoil the airflow over the wings and thus to reduce wing lift. Raised spoilers also generate more drag, thereby giving an aerodynamic braking effect. The disrupted airflow buffets the aircraft structure, which can often be felt by the passengers in the cabin.

This RJ100 has just landed and its spoilers are still extended.

Why would we want to reduce lift and increase drag? Suppose we are descending with our engines at idle thrust (thrust levers fully back) at normal descent speed. This configuration will give us a descent gradient of about 1:20. What if we need to increase our gradient? One answer would be to lower the aircraft's nose, but of course this will also increase our forward speed. If we don't want excess speed (perhaps we are approaching to land) then we must find other means to reduce lift and increase drag. In this case we would pull back the speedbrake lever. The extra drag of the spoilers will try to slow us down. It could be that this might be just what we need. Alternatively, we can maintain speed by lowering the nose, which will of course steepen the descent gradient.

To summarise: the spoilers are used to assist in the control of vertical flight path and forward speed. Remember too that control wheel lateral movement also raises the spoilers on the down-going wing to assist with roll control.

Stabilizer trim

It is clear that the effective mass of the aircraft and its load (in scientific terms, its centre of gravity) must be coincident with the effective lift force generated by the wings. If the **centre of gravity (CG)** is ahead of the lift force the aircraft will be nose heavy and if it is to the rear of the lift force the aircraft will be tail heavy. In other words the aircraft will be **out of trim**.

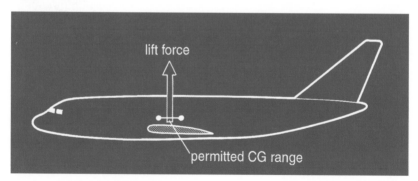

Fig. 13. Permitted range of CG locations.

Of course, it is impossible to achieve exact coincidence. Every person on board the aircraft would have to be precisely weighed and seated accordingly (like balancing a see-saw). And what about the baggage, freight and catering equipment? Not to mention passengers and crew moving up and down the cabin during flight.

In practical terms, the solution to this problem is to permit a **range** of CG locations, so that a small degree of nose or tail heaviness can be tolerated. And no doubt we can use the control wheel to hold the nose in its proper attitude so that the elevators generate an opposing tailplane force.

But this brings a new problem. Suppose the pilot has pulled the wheel back to compensate for nose heaviness. Suppose now he or she needs to raise the nose to a higher attitude. Will there be enough elevator movement left to do this?

You can probably see now the value of an adjustable tailplane. Rather than use the elevators to counter the nose heaviness, why not adjust the tailplane angle to generate the tailplane force? Now the elevators can revert to their 'neutral' position, restoring full authority to the control wheel.

Fig. 14. Nose heaviness countered by (1) elevators and (2) stabilizer trim.

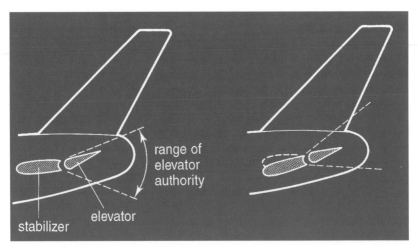

How is this achieved in practice? Any time the pilot has to move the control wheel forward or back to displace the elevators, an opposing bias is applied. The bias tries to restore the wheel to its central position and hence the elevators to their neutral position. The pilot will detect this bias as a push or pull force needed to hold the wheel in the selected position.

By pressing the **stabilizer trim** switch on the control wheel up or down, the pilot can remove the push or pull force so that the nose will remain in the chosen attitude even if the pilot takes his or her hands off the control wheel. The stabilizer trim switch is of course adjusting the angle of the tailplane. When the control wheel force has been removed the elevators are neutral. The aircraft will maintain its pitch attitude 'hands off' and is now **in trim**.

Taxiing

By now we know a fair amount about controlling the aircraft in flight. What about manoeuvring it on the ground? Not surprisingly, airliners are designed to be easy to control in the air, their intended environment. On the ground they are more cumbersome. The Boeing 767, for example, is over 50 metres from nose to tail, which is equivalent to the length of several articulated trucks.

On the ground, speed is controlled by engine thrust and wheel brakes. Great care is needed to move these machines around safely. A fully laden 767 may weigh 180 tonnes or so, which is a lot of inertia. To start it rolling from a rest position is a delicate operation. It is no good applying a big chunk of engine thrust. Certainly the aircraft will move, but in the process any loose objects behind it – baggage trolleys, steps, vehicles, people – will be blown over by the blast from the engines. Thrust must be kept to the minimum necessary. Patience and anticipation are required.

To slow the beast down once it is rolling the pilot retards the thrust levers and presses the upper portions of the rudder pedals. The left pedal is connected to the brakes on the left mainwheels and the right pedal to the right brakes. Overuse of the brakes during taxiing when the aircraft is heavily laden can overheat the wheels to the extent that their tyres deflate, another reason for careful co-ordination of use of thrust and brakes.

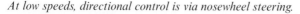

At low speeds, directional control is via nosewheel steering.

Steering is achieved primarily with the tiller handles located to the side of the pilots' seats. Tiller movement is conveyed by cable linkage to hydraulic actuators on the nosewheel leg which turn the wheels left or right. Negotiating a 90° corner on a taxiway requires a high level of concentration. It won't do to steer the flight deck along the taxiway centreline, because the mainwheels will run well to the inside of the turn and the inside wheels may even run off the paved surface. Instead, the same technique is used as for long road vehicles. That is, the nose of the aircraft is made to track to the outside of the centreline so that the mainwheels stay close to it.

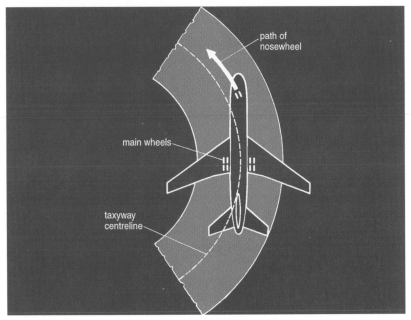

Fig. 15. Taxiing round a corner.

The tightest turn is achieved with the tiller at maximum deflection. If an even tighter turn is necessary the pilot can use **differential thrust**, in other words, increasing thrust on the 'outside' engine. Differential braking (applying either the left or right wheel brakes) will also turn the aircraft. However, this technique puts strain on the tyres and landing gear and so is only used as a last resort, for example on a slippery surface if nosewheel steering is ineffective.

On most airliners, limited nosewheel steering is also applied when the rudder pedals themselves are moved. To summarise: if a gentle left turn is required, move the left rudder pedal forward. If a tighter turn is required, turn the tiller to the left. To tighten the turn further, apply thrust on the right engine.

Thai Airways 747-400 just airborne.

The take-off

Now we know how to control the aircraft on the ground and in the air. Let's put the two ingredients together to fly a take-off. From now on we have to think of our two-pilot crew as having specific roles. We will call the pilot actually in physical control of the aircraft (either the captain or the copilot) the **pilot flying (PF)**. His or her colleague is the **pilot not flying (PNF)**.

To start the manoeuvre, PF taxies the aircraft onto the runway **threshold** (the start of the runway) using the 'long vehicle' technique, so that when the nose swings round to line up with the runway direction the main wheels straddle the **centreline**, marked as a dotted white line.

Now PF pushes the thrust levers forward until the gauges show that take-off thrust has been achieved. A big jet engine can develop about 30 tonnes of thrust and so acceleration is sprightly. PF will concentrate on keeping the aircraft running straight along the centreline, using the rudder pedals (but not the brakes!). Initially the steering is through the nosewheel steering mechanism but as airspeed builds up the rudder itself becomes effective. (Here is an occasion where the rudder *is* controlling aircraft heading.)

PNF will be monitoring that PF is keeping straight and that all the engine gauge readings remain satisfactory. Both pilots will make frequent checks of their airspeed indicators. The captain will have his or her hands on the thrust levers until 'V_1' speed. (We'll come onto that later.) At 'rotation speed' PF pulls the control wheel back to lift, or **rotate**, the nose to the take-off attitude, typically 15° above the horizon. During rotation, the angle of attack of the wings increases and so the lift they generate also increases. As the attitude passes about 10° the lift force will exceed the aircraft's mass and the wheels will leave the ground. We're flying!

As soon as the instruments confirm that the aircraft is climbing PNF selects the landing gear lever up. The hydraulic system will retract the gear. Now PF concentrates on adjusting pitch attitude to maintain the correct initial climb speed. Any turning required will be done by bank inputs from the control wheel (*not* the rudder!) PNF will be monitoring PF's performance through his or her own instruments and keeping one eye on the engine gauges. At a safe height either PF or PNF will bring the thrust levers back to climb thrust (to save engine wear-and-tear). PF will lower the nose slightly to accelerate the aircraft so that PNF can gradually retract the flaps.

Now the aircraft is in the 'clean' configuration (landing gear and flaps retracted) and will remain so for the remainder of the climb, the cruise and the descent until the approach to landing commences.

STOP!

Suppose something goes wrong during the take-off run. Can the pilots stop the aircraft without running off the end of the runway? This is where the V_1 speed mentioned above comes into play. The V_1 speed is one of the **V-speeds** which we'll look at in more detail when we consider aircraft performance.

If a malfunction occurs during the take-off run before V_1 has been reached, the Captain must decide whether to carry out the **rejected take-off (RTO)** procedure. The RTO procedure entails retarding the thrust levers, applying reverse thrust and wheel brakes and raising the spoilers (using the speedbrake lever). The raised spoilers reduce wing lift, thereby putting more weight onto the mainwheels and thus increasing the effectiveness of the wheel brakes.

In order to achieve the RTO configuration as quickly as possible some of these functions occur automatically. For example, on the Boeing 767 the action of closing the thrust levers and applying reverse thrust also engages the wheel brakes and raises the spoilers without pilot input.

At the start of the take-off run it is likely that the captain would reject the take-off for any malfunction, even a minor one. But as the speed approaches V_1 it is safer to continue the take-off unless a serious problem occurs. After V_1 the pilots are committed to continue the take-off, because there may now be insufficient runway remaining to come to a stop.

Fine, you say, but suppose an engine fails just after V_1. What happens then? The answer is that the aircraft will continue its take-off. Here is a comforting thought for all air travellers. *Every take-off in every airliner is based on the possibility that an engine may fail at any time.* If the failure occurs before V_1 there will be enough runway left to stop. If it occurs after V_1 the aircraft can complete its take-off and fly, albeit with degraded climb performance. On shorter runways it may be necessary to restrict the aircraft's load to make sure that it has this capability. In the past you may have had to suffer the inconvenience of a refuelling stop during your travels by air. This might well have been as a result of reducing the fuel load in order to guarantee the engine-failure perform-ance during take-off.

The landing

Well, we got the beast into the air. How are we going to get it back down on the ground in one piece? First of all it has to be slowed down, ini-tially to the minimum flaps-up speed. Then with perhaps ten or twelve miles to go to touchdown, the flaps are partially extended and speed correspondingly reduced. We are now in the 'intermediate approach' configuration, with landing gear still retracted. Engine thrust is adjust-ed to maintain the intermediate approach speed while pitch inputs are made to control the vertical flight path. The approach angle is a slope of 3°, which equates to 300 feet of height to be lost for every nautical mile flown in the forward direction.

At about five miles from touchdown the landing gear is extended and the flaps fully lowered. This is the 'final approach' configuration. Airspeed is allowed to reduce to the correct final approach speed and then thrust is increased to maintain this speed. Why is the increase in thrust necessary? You can probably guess the answer – it is to counter-act the drag arising from the extended gear and fully lowered flaps.

Now PF is working hard. With control wheel inputs he or she must maintain the correct vertical flight path to the aiming point for touch-down, which is 1,000 feet (300 metres) beyond the runway threshold, simultaneously adjusting engine thrust as necessary to hold the correct final approach speed. If the speed drops too low the loss of lift and high drag can bring about a dangerous increase in sink rate. On the other hand too much speed will increase the length of runway required to land the aircraft and slow it down to taxiing speed.

And while doing all of this, PF must also keep the aircraft lined up with the runway centreline, using bank inputs to control heading. You can be sure that PNF will be monitoring attentively and will have no compunction about calling out deviations from the correct approach path and speed.

But supposing the wind is blowing from one side? It's a good point. Very rarely does the wind blow in the same direction as the runway is pointing. If it's not strong there's not too much of a problem, but a strong crosswind … Let's leave crosswinds for the moment. Things are busy enough as it is. Now the runway is approaching fast and although the aircraft structure and landing gear are built to withstand ground impact at the approach rate of descent, the nerves of the humans inside are not.

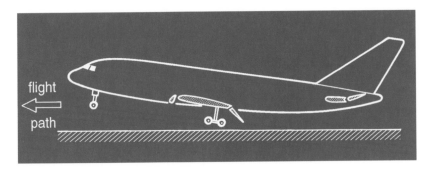

Fig. 16. Landing attitude.

And so, when the aircraft is about 20 feet above the runway, PF must raise the nose, or flare, to arrest the descent rate, simultaneously retarding the thrust levers to idle. If the flare is done properly the aircraft will attain an almost level flight path in its landing attitude just above the runway. The flare manoeuvre is judged visually, rather than by reference to the instruments, although on some aircraft types automatic height call-outs from the **radio altimeter** (which we'll look at later) may be helpful.

The aircraft will now sink onto its mainwheels. As soon as it has touched down the speedbrake lever automatically moves back to raise the spoilers. Now PF must apply reverse thrust and move the control wheel forward to bring the nose gently down and so fly the nosewheel onto the runway. The wheel brakes are applied either automatically or by input from PF (on the rudder pedal top portions). To keep straight during the landing roll requires rudder inputs (the control wheel will no longer be of any use). As the aircraft slows to taxiing speed the reverse thrust is cancelled and the wheel braking reduced as appropriate. The aircraft is now a creature of the ground again. Phew!

Varig MD-11 at the point of touchdown.

The go-around

It could be that for some reason the aircraft is not able to complete the landing manoeuvre. For example, the pilots may consider that the aircraft is not flying a stable final approach path and speed, or perhaps the runway is blocked by another aircraft or ground vehicle.

In cases such as these the approach must be abandoned by means of the **go-around (GA)** procedure. The manoeuvre is done in two stages. Firstly, PF advances the thrust levers to full thrust and raises the nose to the GA pitch attitude, usually 15° (just like the take-off). PNF will partially retract the flaps and, when the instruments confirm that the aircraft is climbing away, retract the landing gear. Then at a safe height (again, just like the take-off) the thrust is reduced to climb thrust, PF lowers the nose to accelerate and PNF completes the flap retraction.

What about that crosswind?

During the take-off run, any crosswind will act on the fin and make the aircraft's nose tend to weathercock into wind. So a crosswind from the right will cause the aircraft's nose to try to wander to the right. No problem, because we can use the rudder pedals to compensate for any tendency to stray from the centreline and so keep the aircraft running straight.

If the crosswind is strong, the only other thing we need to do is to hold the control wheel 'into wind'. So in our crosswind from the right we should hold the wheel to the right. This will prevent any tendency for the 'into wind' wing to lift prematurely prior to rotation. Once in the air the flight controls are used normally.

Fig. 17. Approach for crosswind landing.

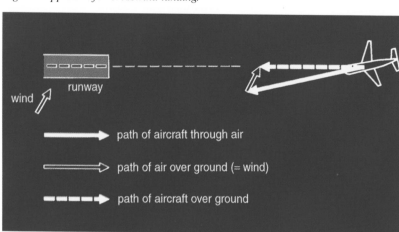

The situation is different on the approach to landing. Having lined up with the runway we must use bank inputs to choose a heading which compensates for the sideways drift. The aircraft's nose will be pointing slightly 'into wind' but it is important to remember that *the airflow past the aircraft is symmetrical, even though its path over the ground is not in the same direction as the nose is pointing.* In other words, the flight controls are being used normally, with rudder and control wheel central except for roll inputs to adjust heading.

If the crosswind is not strong then we can use the standard flare and touchdown technique. This means of course that because of the drift the mainwheels will contact the ground at a slight angle, which the tyres and landing gear can easily withstand. After touchdown the rudder pedals are used to straighten the aircraft and then stop any weather-cocking tendency during the landing roll.

For a strong crosswind the standard technique will not do, because the sideways strain on the tyres and landing gear is unacceptably high. In this situation we use normal control inputs until the flare manoeuvre has been accomplished. Then, just before touchdown, we use the rudder pedals to swing the nose into line with the runway so that on ground contact the wheels are pointing straight ahead, or nearly so.

5
Performance

We know quite a bit now. We know how to make the aircraft take-off, climb, fly level, turn, descend and land. Now we'll turn our attention to what it can actually do in specific terms. How fast can it fly? How high? How far? How much payload (passengers, baggage and freight) can it carry?

Take-off performance

Let's start on the ground and look at the aircraft's take-off performance capabilities. Here's a typical problem. We need to fly our Boeing 767-300 from Birmingham, England to Miami, Florida. We can expect to consume around 45 to 50 tonnes of fuel, depending on circumstances. Can we make the flight non-stop? Bear in mind that it would be foolhardy to arrive with fuel tanks nearly empty. Common sense – and regulations – demand that a reserve be carried. So the answer to the question is: maybe. It depends on:

- the mass of the payload
- exactly how much fuel is required (how do we calculate that?)
- the length of the runway available
- the air temperature and pressure at the airport
- the direction and strength of the wind at the airport

Perhaps it is not surprising that runway length is a major factor in determining how much mass the aircraft can lift. The longer the runway, the higher can be the rotation speed and therefore the greater the lift generated at lift-off. Here are some runway lengths at British airports:

- London (Heathrow): 3,900 metres (12,800 feet) and 3,660 m (12,000 ft) (two runways)
- London (Gatwick): 3,320 m (10,890 ft)
- London (Stansted): 3,050 m (10,000 ft)
- Manchester: 3,050 m (10,000 ft) and 3,050 m (10,000 ft) (two runways)
- East Midlands: 2,890 m (9,480 ft)
- Belfast: 2,780 m (9,120 ft)
- Glasgow: 2,660 m (8,720 ft)
- Birmingham: 2,610 m (8,560 ft)
- Edinburgh: 2,560 m (8,400 ft)
- Cardiff: 2,350 m (7,710 ft)
- Newcastle: 2,350 m (7,710 ft)

- Leeds Bradford: 2,260 m (7,410 ft)
- London (Luton): 2,160 m (7,080 ft)
- Bristol: 2,010 m (6,590 ft)

To a certain degree shortness of runway can be compensated for by using a greater (more extended) flap setting for take-off, so that the lift required can be generated at lower rotation speed. But there is a snag. Remember that we have to allow for the case of engine failure. The greater flap setting, besides yielding more lift, will also incur the penalty of more drag. So the aircraft's climb performance with an engine failed will not be as good as with a reduced flap setting, which means some of the extra mass-lifting capability will be lost again.

To summarise: the longer the runway, the greater the mass we can lift off it, up to the maximum permitted **structural** take-off mass specified in the aircraft's Flight Manual.

A related factor is the nature of the terrain surrounding the airport. Consider the case of Malaga in Spain. The runway direction is southeast–northwest. The airport lies on the coast, one end of the runway is pointing out to sea and the other towards mountainous terrain. Take-off performance to the southeast, climbing out over the sea, is good. But in the opposite direction maximum take-off mass allowed is severely limited by the terrain, because, as always, we have to allow for the possibility of engine failure just after V_1. The aircraft must be able to clear the terrain with an engine failed.

Now we must consider air temperature and pressure at the airport. Why? Because the lifting ability of the wings and the thrust available from the engines both depend on air density, which in turn depends on temperature and pressure. Higher density improves both lift and thrust. The lower the air temperature, and the greater its pressure, the more dense is the air and the better the aircraft will perform.

Lastly, the wind. Suppose we are in position on the runway threshold, lined up for take-off. If the wind is blowing towards us we will have a 'bonus' extra airspeed equal to the speed of the wind. The wings will have already started to generate lift even though the aircraft is stationary. In other words, when we are accelerating along the runway we will reach rotation speed on our airspeed indicators sooner than if there was no wind, thereby requiring less runway for take-off. Putting this another way, we can achieve a higher rotation speed on a particular runway if the wind is blowing against us and therefore we can lift more mass. If you have trouble visualising this concept, imagine that the wind speed equals the aircraft's rotation speed. We wouldn't need a runway at all! The aircraft could take-off vertically.

So, take-off performance is enhanced if we have a **headwind** and reduced if we have a **tailwind**. In a crosswind, we must split the wind into its head- or tailwind component and its crosswind component. Of course, the crosswind component will neither enhance nor degrade the take-off performance.

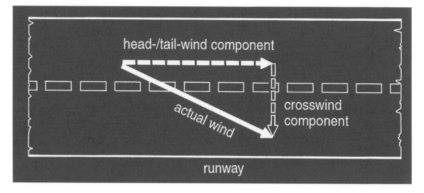

Fig. 18. Wind components.

The pilots on our Birmingham–Miami flight will need to refer to the aircraft's **Take-Off Performance Data** (in book or electronic data base form) which details the maximum permitted take-off mass for any particular runway at any particular airport for the actual conditions of air temperature, sea level air pressure (sea level being the datum) and head- or tailwind component. Also stated will be the appropriate flap setting for take-off.

Here's a winter's day at Birmingham:
* temperature: 4°C
* pressure: 1,023 millibars (sea level)
* headwind: 10 knots

The take-off performance data gives the following figures for the south-east facing runway:
* max. take-off mass: 178,200 kilograms (178.2 tonnes)
* V_1: 161 knots; V_R: 163 knots; V_2: 170 knots

The zero-fuel mass (ZFM) of the aircraft is its total mass except for fuel. It includes the aircraft itself, its equipment, the crew and the payload. On today's Birmingham-Miami flight the pilots have been informed by the traffic office that the ZFM is 126,100 kilograms (126.1 tonnes). Subtracting this figure from the take-off performance data figure above leaves 52,100 kilograms (52.1 tonnes) available for fuel.

If the fuel required is less than the availability figure then we can fly non-stop. If it is greater, we have problems. We must either reduce the aircraft mass (perhaps off-loading non-important freight) or else make a refuelling stop en route.

Here's a midsummer day:
- temperature: 26°C
- pressure: 1,003 mb (sea level)
- headwind: 0 knots

The take-off performance data gives the following figures:
- max. take-off mass: 167,300 kg
- V_1: 154 knots; V_R: 157 knots; V_2: 165 knots

It appears that the chances of making a non-stop flight are reduced. However, on this particular day the aircraft's zero fuel mass might be different, as might the fuel required. We'll look at fuel calculations later on.

What about these V-speeds? We are already familiar with V_1, the maximum speed at which a rejected take-off can be initiated without running off the end of the runway. V_R is the rotation speed, when PF lifts the nose for take-off. V_2 is the **take-off safety speed**. We're back to this engine failure business. After V_1, remember, the pilots must continue the take-off. Once airborne, V_2 is the speed to fly with an engine failed. It gives a margin of about 20% over the stalling speed and ensures that the aircraft will achieve an adequate climb gradient. This speed is flown, with landing gear retracted of course, until nearby obstacles and terrain are cleared, after which PF can lower the nose to accelerate and PNF can retract the flaps, as in the normal take-off.

A reminder: airspeed indicators are calibrated in **knots**, which are nautical miles per hour. (One nautical miles equals 1,852 metres or 6,076 feet, which is 15% greater than a statute mile.) A frequent question is: what speed does the aircraft take-off at? We know now that the answer is not a fixed speed, but depends on circumstances. In the first example quoted above V_R was 163 knots, which equates to 187 mph.

Save the engines!

The discussion above assumes that for take-off the engines are developing **rated** thrust, which is the maximum thrust achievable. Aircraft engines are like all machines – if treated with consideration they will reward the operator with longer service and greater reliability.

Usually the take-pff performance available from the aircraft is well in excess of that required, even allowing for engine failure. When this is the case, we can set the engines to less than maximum thrust and still achieve normal safety margins. In other words the pilots can use **derated** thrust. The Take-Off Performance Data will therefore have figures for rated thrust and also for various derated thrust settings. Other factors being equal, pilots will normally choose the lowest derated thrust permissible if this option is available to them.

This British Airways 747-400 is powered by Rolls-Royce RB211 engines.

Climb

After take-off, with all engines operating normally, PF flies a pitch attitude which gives an initial climb speed between V_2 + 15 and V_2 + 25
knots. The gradient of climb will be quite steep at this point. This is
desirable because it assists with noise abatement by taking the noise of
the engines away from the ground as quickly as possible.

Following flap retraction, PF must choose an appropriate climb
speed. With no terrain constraints, he or she will normally accelerate to
economy climb speed (using pitch attitude to control speed, of course,

The Airbus A300 is still in service with many airlines.

Some DC-10s have been converted into freighters

Multiple landing gear units on the 747 spread the aircraft's mass evenly over the ground.

with the engines set to climb thrust). For the Boeing 767 the economy climb speed is typically in the region of 310 knots.

For terrain clearance, the climb speed is held back to minimum flaps-up speed to retain a good gradient. For the 767 the minimum flaps-up speed will range from about 220 to 260 knots, depending on aircraft mass. Once the high terrain has been over-flown, PF can accelerate to economy speed. We'll find out exactly what 'economy speed' means later on.

As we climb into the upper atmosphere we find that the aircraft's climb performance gradually diminishes because the air density reduces, as does its temperature (which partially offsets the density reduction). At 37,000 feet, a typical cruising height for jet airliners, the air density is only about 30% of its sea level value and the temperature around -56°C.

True airspeed

The airspeed indicator works by measuring the pressure build-up in a hollow probe facing into the airflow. If the air density reduces, the pressure build-up sensed is less than at normal density. In other words, *as height is gained during the climb the airspeed indicator progressively under-reads.* At 37,000 feet, for example, an **indicated airspeed** (IAS) of 260 knots equates to a **true airspeed (TAS)** of 460 knots. TAS is the actual speed of the aircraft through the air. Since the climb is flown at a fixed **IAS**, the TAS increases as height is gained.

The aerodynamic characteristics of the aircraft relate to IAS rather than TAS (which is why we use a fixed IAS for the climb). One consequence of this is that the manufacturers will specify a maximum allowed IAS, to protect the aircraft from excessive aerodynamic stresses. For the Boeing 767 this speed is 360 knots.

Mach number

If we set the engines to maximum thrust, how high could the aircraft go before it stopped climbing? If we tried to find out we would start to encounter an inexplicable buffeting. Reducing the airspeed (by raising the nose) would stop the buffeting – for a while – but as we climbed higher it would start again. So, we could progressively reduce airspeed, couldn't we? Yes, but only until we approached stalling speed.

Fig. 19. Buffet boundary, with maximum permitted IAS, Mach number and altitude.

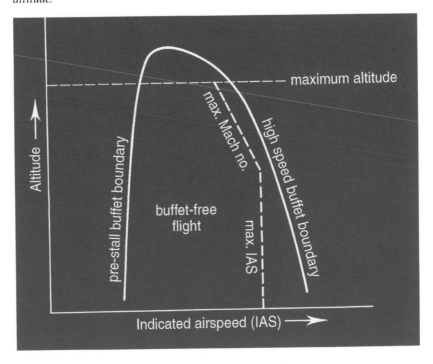

What we have discovered here is the **buffet boundary**. Inside the buffet boundary the aircraft flies normally. At or outside the boundary the aircraft will experience either **high-speed buffet** or **pre-stall buffet**, the latter caused by the airflow breaking away from the wings as the stalling angle is approached.

The high-speed buffet arises because the aircraft is approaching the **speed of sound**, which is simply the speed at which the individual molecules of air are naturally moving about. At **subsonic** speeds the air molecules can move out of the way as the aircraft passes through them. But as we nudge the speed of sound it is more difficult for the molecules to move away and so a **shock wave** builds up ahead of the aircraft. This shock wave is felt as buffet. Aircraft which cruise at high subsonic speeds are designed with their wings and tail surfaces swept back at an angle. Although aesthetically pleasing, the real purpose of sweepback is not to improve the aircraft's looks but to delay the onset of shock waves.

Now we can answer the question: the aircraft can keep climbing until it is experiencing simultaneous pre-stall and high-speed buffeting. It is physically impossible for it to fly any higher.

If we ignore the high-speed buffeting and try to fly faster (by lowering the nose, for example) the buffeting will get worse. The aircraft will become uncontrollable and its structure may be overstressed and perhaps damaged. Therefore, besides the maximum permitted IAS, the manufacturers also impose a maximum permissible speed based on **Mach number**. An aircraft's Mach number is expressed as the ratio of its

In the upper atmosphere water vapour from the engine exhausts instantly condenses into ice crystals, forming contrails.

true airspeed to the speed of sound. The Mach number is one of the parameters displayed on the pilots' instrument panels.

As we climb at constant indicated airspeed, then, the true airspeed and the Mach number gradually increase. When the Mach indication has reached the economy reading we adjust pitch attitude to fly this Mach number, with the result that the indicated airspeed gradually decreases. For the Boeing 767 the economy climb speed is around 0.80 Mach, meaning that its true airspeed is 80% of the speed of sound. The maximum permitted Mach number is 0.84, which is comfortably inside the buffet boundary.

At 37,000 feet the speed of sound is about 580 knots (670 mph). A Mach number of 0.80 therefore equates to about 460 knots true airspeed (530 mph).

To give further protection the manufacturer will specify the maximum permitted altitude (meaning height above sea level), which again will be comfortably below that actually achievable. The maximum permitted altitude depends on aircraft mass. Why? Because greater mass requires higher angle of attack to generate the necessary lift, which increases the stalling speed and therefore reduces the buffet-free speed range. Therefore the heavier the aircraft, the lower will be its maximum permitted altitude.

Cruise

Well, we've looked at *maximum* permitted altitude and Mach number. The next thing to decide is: what is the *optimum* altitude to fly? What is the optimum speed? The main factors to consider here are fuel mileage and crew and maintenance costs.

Flying for maximum range

If we measured how many miles we could fly on a given amount of fuel at various indicated airspeeds we would find that there was one particular speed where the mileage was greatest. The higher we fly, of course, the greater is the *true* airspeed related to this indicated airspeed, which means we could go even farther. However, as we approach the maximum permitted altitude the overall efficiency of the aircraft begins to diminish and so the mileage suffers. For the Boeing 767 the optimum altitude to fly is about 3,000 feet below maximum permitted and the optimum speed is in the region of Mach 0.80. As fuel is consumed on a long flight so the aircraft's mass decreases and the optimum altitude increases. To determine the actual optimum speed and altitude in the prevailing circumstances the pilots will refer to the aircraft's **Flight Management Computer (FMC)** – which we'll look at later – or else to tables in the Flight Manual.

Flying for maximum economy

Besides the consumption of fuel there are other costs involved in the operation of airliners. The crew must be paid and so must the maintenance costs. Both of these factors dictate minimising the time the aircraft is actually in flight, which means flying it as fast as possible. But flying faster than speed for maximum range will increase fuel consumption, the cost of the extra fuel offsetting the gains of time reduction. And so a compromise is required to determine the best **economy** speed. This speed will minimise the overall cost of operating the flight.

By and large, fuel cost is the major factor and so the economy speed mentioned previously will not be much greater than the speed for maximum range. Again, the FMC will give the actual figure.

Swept-back wings and tail surfaces allow the modern jetliner to cruise at high Mach numbers (Britannia Airways 757).

Flying for maximum endurance

In today's crowded skies it is not unusual for an airliner to approach its destination only to find that there is a queue for landing. Normally, waiting aircraft are directed by air traffic control to a **holding pattern**, where they follow a racecourse-shaped path. Now our concern is not to fly as *far* as possible, but to make the fuel last *as long as possible*. To do this we fly at speed for **maximum endurance**. Usually this speed approximates to the minimum flaps-up speed.

Descent

As the destination airport approaches, where should we start our descent and at what speed should we descend? For jet airliners, the most efficient profile is one in which the engines are brought back to idle thrust and pitch attitude used to fly economy descent speed. For the Boeing 767 this typically means starting off at 0.80 Mach. As we lose height of course the indicated airspeed builds up. When it reaches economy speed we abandon Mach number and use pitch attitude to maintain this speed, typically 290 knots for the 767.

Bearing in mind that the glide angle for most airliners is about 1:20, we can see that from a cruising altitude of 37,000 feet, the descent should be started at twenty times this figure, which is about 120 nautical miles from touchdown.

Landing

Our main concern is length of runway required. The final approach is flown at a few knots above V_{ref}, the reference speed for landing, the idea being that when the flare manoeuvre is complete just prior to touchdown the speed will have dropped to V_{ref}. V_{ref} is calculated as 30% above stalling speed in the landing configuration (landing gear extended and flaps fully down). We already know that the heavier the aircraft, the greater is its stalling speed. Therefore V_{ref} is greater. Additionally the brakes take longer to slow down a heavier aircraft. Both of these factors mean that the heavier the aircraft, the greater the runway length required for landing.

A headwind will reduce speed over the ground and therefore reduce the length required and a tailwind will increase it. The Flight Manual will specify the distance required for any combination of aircraft mass and wind component. This figure includes a safety margin and assumes the use of maximum wheel braking. If the length of runway available exceeds that required it is normal practice to go easy on the brakes in order to reduce wear. Retardation is assisted by use of reverse thrust.

A typical landing mass for the Boeing 767 is 130 tonnes (130,000 kilograms), giving a V_{ref} of 137 knots (158 mph). With a calm wind the corresponding landing distance required is 1,790 metres (5,880 feet). This figure includes the 300 metres (1,000 feet) between the runway threshold and the touchdown point.

The air data computer

Several of the flight parameter indications are derived from the measurement of air pressure. We have already looked at the airspeed indicator, which compares ambient, or **static** air pressure against that sensed by a probe facing into the airflow (which is called **pitot** pressure). The altimeter works by measurement of static pressure alone, on the basis that the higher we go, the less is the air pressure. The vertical speed indicator measures the rate of change of static pressure as we climb or descend. In small aircraft these pressure inputs drive the instruments directly. In modern airliners the inputs are fed into an **air data computer**, which converts them into the presentation on the pilots' instrument panels.

6
Navigation

In the fledgling days of aviation navigation was by visual reference, matching features on the ground with their representation on maps. The pilots of light aircraft still use this technique today, but it is not always an easy task, for example in poor visibility or at night. Even in good weather there can be difficulties. If you're following a road or railway, how do you know it's the right one? Suppose there are no line features to follow. How do work out what heading to fly to get to where you want to go? What happens if the wind is blowing you off course? How do you navigate over the sea?

Airliners have to fly according to their published schedules, regardless of weather, often over deserts and oceans. Not so long ago, aeronautical navigation was sufficiently specialised to require the presence of a person on the flight deck for just this function. The **navigator** calculated aircraft position using a combination of techniques, primarily by means of radio equipment, which measured bearings to beacons or how long it took the signals to arrive at the aircraft. If the sky was visible the sun and stars could also be used to determine position. For

Fig. 20. Compass directions.

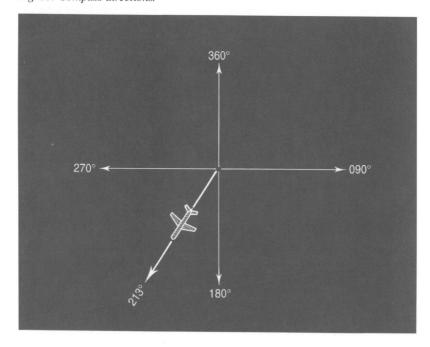

the pilots, then, the heading to fly was that which the navigator worked out for them.

Nowadays navigators have all but vanished from airliner flight decks. Radio beacons are still in use, but interpretation of their signals is much easier, enabling the pilots to take over the duty of navigation. The task is further simplified by the **flight management computer** fitted to most modern airliners, which we'll look at later.

Direction

Some things haven't changed. The reference for heading is still **magnetic north**, which is the direction a suspended magnetised needle points in. The horizontal situation indicator (HSI) uses magnetic north as its datum. Heading is expressed in degrees as a three figure group. Thus east is 090°, south 180°, west 270° and north 360° (rather than 000°). So an aircraft flying a heading of 213°, for example, is pointing slightly south of southwest. All aircraft, even the largest jumbos, are equipped with a back-up magnetic compass which needs no power supply, just like a car compass (although more accurate).

Latitude and longitude

We need a reference system so that we can describe the exact location of any point on the earth's surface. The two datums are the **equator** and the **zero** (or **prime**) **meridian**. The equator is the datum for **latitude**. The latitude of any point on the earth's surface is expressed in terms of degrees, minutes (and tenths of a minute) north or south of the equator. (One minute of latitude equals one sixtieth of a degree.) For example, the North Pole is at latitude 90° north (expressed as N9000.0) and the South Pole at 90° south (S9000.0). Birmingham airport is at latitude N5227.4, meaning 52° 27.4' north of the equator.

The zero meridian is the datum for **longitude**. It is a line joining the north and south poles, passing through Greenwich in London. The longitude of any point on the earth's surface is expressed in degrees, minutes and tenths west or east of the zero meridian. The meridian on the opposite side of the earth is at longitude 180° west, and of course also at 180° east. Birmingham airport is at longitude W00145.2, meaning 1° 45.2' west of the zero meridian. Some other examples:

- Miami Airport, Florida: N2547.1 W08016.6
- Perth Airport, Australia: S3156.8 E11557.5

Radio aids

As mentioned above, radio aids to navigation have been in use for many years, and will probably continue to give service for quite a while yet.

Some of these beacons transmit in the medium frequency range, but many of them are being withdrawn. Others transmit in the very high frequency (VHF) range, such as the VHF omni radio (VOR). Bearings from these beacons can be displayed on the pilots' horizontal situation indicators. VORs are often supplemented with distance measuring equipment (DME) beacons, transmitting in the ultra high frequency (UHF) range. Aircraft fitted with DME receivers can thus indicate to the pilots their distance to or from these beacons.

Many of the world's airways are still marked out by radio beacons, allowing all-weather navigation by aircraft fitted only with the equipment described above. In this case the task is straightforward because the pilots can navigate directly from one beacon to the next.

Track and groundspeed

To fly direct to a radio beacon is simple then, isn't it, because we just have to point the aircraft's nose straight at it. But suppose there is a crosswind. The aircraft will be blown off course, won't it? Here we are in the same situation as on the approach for a crosswind landing.

Fig. 21. Heading, drift and track.

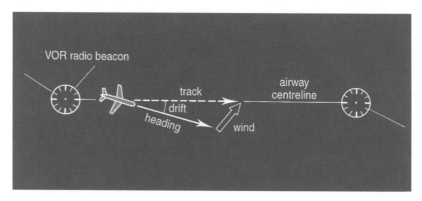

We must pick a heading slightly into wind so that the aircraft's **track** (its path over the ground) is in the right direction. The **drift** is the difference between heading and track. If the wind has a headwind component our **groundspeed** will be less than our true airspeed. A tailwind component will give a groundspeed higher than TAS, as in the example shown.

Inertial reference systems

The **inertial reference system (IRS)** is a navigational device fitted in many modern airliners, particularly those engaged in long-haul flying. It is normal practice to install three systems in each aircraft. Each IRS is an assembly of laser gyroscopes and accelerometers. Before take-off the pilots input the aircraft's location (latitude and longitude) into the IRSs. Thereafter the gyros and accelerometers measure aircraft movement and the IRSs use this information to compute present position, track and groundspeed. The gyros also feed attitude signals to the pilots' attitude indicators and heading signals into the horizontal situation indicators.

One reason for multiple installation is for comparison purposes. The three IRSs compare their computations and if any of the three disagree from the other two they will alert the pilots. The second reason is for back-up, so that loss of one or two systems does not leave the aircraft devoid of IRS information. Modern IRSs are incredibly accurate. After a flight of several hours or so it is unusual to see discrepancies of more than one or two nautical miles.

Flight management computers

Most modern jet airliners are now fitted with **flight management computers** (FMCs). The FMC processes performance information and navigational information and displays its calculations to the pilots.

Before take-off the pilots input certain performance data into the FMC, including aircraft zero fuel mass and cost index. The fuel tank quantity readings are sent to the FMC automatically. Thus the FMC knows at all times the total aircraft mass. It uses this data to compute the optimum indicated airspeed and Mach number to fly and the optimum altitude at which to cruise. Modes available to the pilots are: maximum range, maximum endurance or maximum economy. The FMC uses the cost index to make the economy calculations. It will also compute the point at which to initiate descent for landing.

In addition to performance data, the pilots input the planned route into the FMC. The airways to be followed are marked by **waypoints**, which are specific geographic locations defined by latitude and longitude and given 5-letter code names or **designators**. Some waypoints are radio beacons, with 3-letter designators. During flight the FMC displays the route to the pilots in the form of a **track line** on their horizontal situation indicators. The FMCs use the inertial reference systems to display current aircraft position in relation to the planned route. When there are radio beacons within range they also automatically tune these in to check that the IRS position calculations are correct.

Normal practice is for two FMCs to be fitted to the aircraft, each making its calculations independently of the other. One FMC will supply the captain's HSI and the other the copilot's. The FMCs will compare their results and alert the pilots if they are in disagreement.

If one FMC fails, the other is capable of supplying navigational information to both HSIs.

And if both FMCs fail? You can manage without, of course. If you're flying a Boeing 767, climb at 310 knots indicated (engines at climb thrust), switching to Mach 0.80 as you get higher. Choose a cruising altitude between 33,000 and 41,000 feet, depending on aircraft mass (as close as you can get to 3,000 feet below maximum permitted). Cruise at Mach 0.80 (thrust controlling speed now). Divide your altitude in hundreds of feet by a factor of three and this number will be the distance in nautical miles from your destination airport where you should start descending. (This is the familiar 1:20 glide gradient.) So at 41,000 feet you should start your descent at 130-140 miles from the airport. Reduce the engines to idle thrust and descend at – surprise – Mach 0.80 until the airspeed indicator shows 290 knots and then hold this speed. If by comparing current altitude against distance to go you reckon you're descending too steeply or not steeply enough, adjust your vertical profile with engine thrust or speedbrake. Fly 290 knots until you're down to a height of 10,000 feet. Now reduce speed to 250 knots until you get down to about 5,000 feet, when you can slow down further to minimum flaps up speed. The rest you already know.

Fig. 22. HSI displaying route track line.

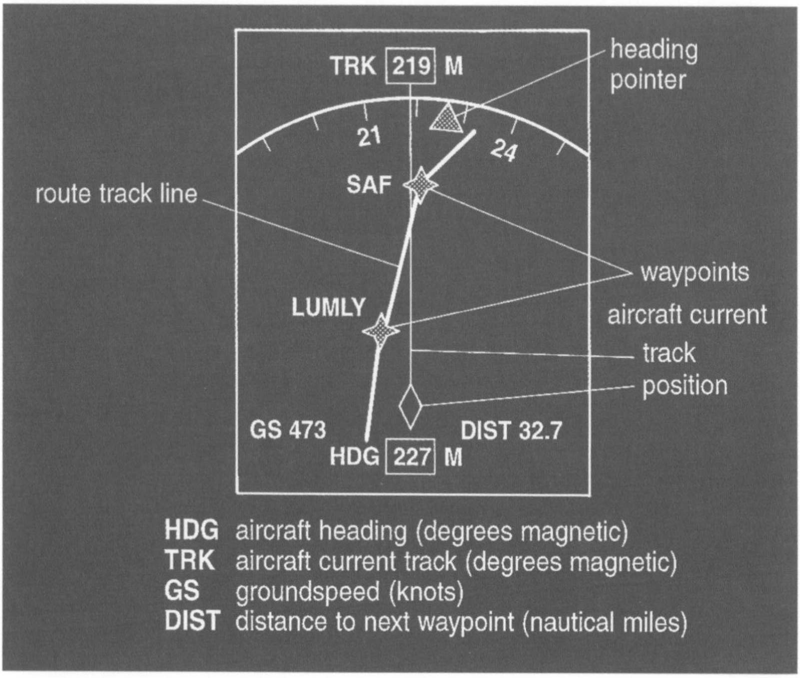

HDG   aircraft heading (degrees magnetic)
TRK   aircraft current track (degrees magnetic)
GS   groundspeed (knots)
DIST   distance to next waypoint (nautical miles)

What about navigation without FMCs? You can manually tune in radio beacons to get bearing and distance information and use the IRSs to cross check your position. Additionally the air traffic controllers on the ground can give you assistance if you need it. (We'll see how later on.)

Charts

The maps used by pilots are called **charts**. As you would expect they differ considerably from road maps. In fact the only geographic features on them are coastlines. Instead, the charts show where the airways are and the location of the waypoints and radio beacons which define the airways. Each airway has its own designator (like road numbers). The bearings (directions) between the beacons or waypoints are shown (in degrees relative to magnetic north) and the distances, in nautical miles, between them. The frequencies on which the beacons transmit are also given. Each beacon identifies itself by transmitting its designator in Morse code, enabling the pilots to confirm that they have tuned in the correct one. Some airways are not predicated on beacons and are therefore only available to aircraft with more sophisticated navigation equipment such as IRSs and FMCs.

The charts also show the boundaries of the airspace divisions where ground control of overflying traffic changes from one agency to another (something else we'll look at in more detail later).

Since aircraft may be flying in cloud or at night, air navigation charts also specify **minimum flight altitudes** (heights above sea level) both on the airways and outside them. These MFAs ensure adequate clearance over terrain and significant obstructions (such as buildings and television masts).

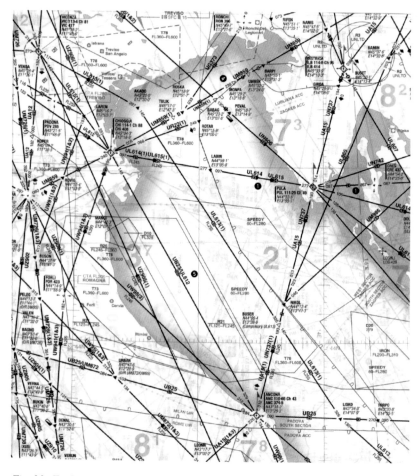

Fig. 23. En Route Navigation Chart.

Instrument landing system

It's all very well, you say, making sure you stay above minimum flight altitude. How are you going to get down for landing? The answer, of course, is a guidance system which allows the aircraft to follow a safe horizontal and vertical flight profile all the way down to the runway.

There are several methods available for safely approaching to land in bad weather or at night, the most widespread being the **instrument landing system (ILS)**. Each ILS installation has two main components, both of which are radio beams, and often an associated distance measuring equipment beacon, which tells the pilots their distance from the runway.

The **localiser** beam is transmitted along the runway centreline and gives left and right guidance on the pilots' HSIs. The **glideslope** beam is

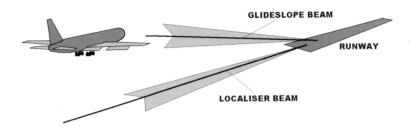

Fig. 24A. ILS installation.

transmitted from the touchdown point on the runway out along the approach at an upward angle of 3°. This beam defines the correct vertical approach path, the pilots' HSIs showing whether the aircraft is above or below the glideslope.

Special landing charts give pilots the details of the ILS installation at the destination airport. Among other things, they show the frequency on which the ILS transmits, the direction of the localiser beam, the terrain surrounding the airport, the elevation (height above sea level) of the run-

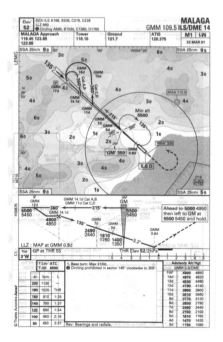

Fig. 24B. ILS chart.

71

During the cruise the pilots must brief themselves on arrival procedures.

way and the route and altitude to fly if for some reason the aircraft cannot land and PF (the pilot flying) has to carry out a go around.

Approach and runway lighting

Having tuned the appropriate frequency on the aircraft's ILS receiver, PF follows the localiser and glideslope indications until he or she can see the **approach lights**. The approach lights are white, laid out in a special pattern showing where the runway will appear when it comes into sight. The **runway lights** have several elements. The runway's edges and its centreline are marked with white lights. The landing threshold (where the runway starts) is indicated by green lights and the far threshold by red lights. Either side of the runway, adjacent to the touchdown point, are located the **precision approach path indicator (PAPI)** lights. If the aircraft is on the correct vertical profile each PAPI set shows two red and two white lights. If the aircraft gets low the indication changes to three reds and one white and if lower still, four reds. If it is too high the PAPIs show three whites and one red, four whites if even higher.

Even in good weather, PF will make use of the ILS and or PAPIs if they are available. Most major airports are equipped with both systems, and many with one or the other. Without ILS glideslope or PAPI assistance it is a more difficult task for pilots to judge and maintain the correct approach path to the correct touchdown point.

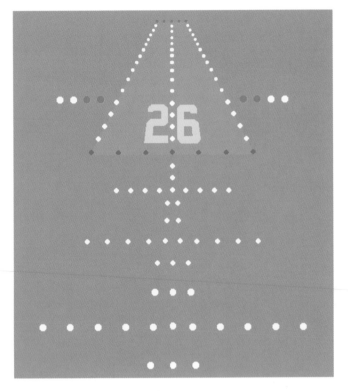

Fig. 25. Approach and runway lighting.

PAPI indications confirm that this crew is following the correct vertical flight path to runway 26L at London Gatwick.

Runway designators

The **runway designator** is determined by the direction in which it points, relative to magnetic north, to the nearest 10°, with the final zero omitted. For example, at London Luton Airport the main runway points in the direction 259° and is therefore designated runway 26. Used in the opposite direction the runway is designated 08 (because it points in the direction 079°). The designators are painted on the runway thresholds in large white numbers.

If the airport has two parallel runways then they are designated L (left) or R (right). The two main runways at Manchester are 06L/24R and 06R/24L.

The future

Along with telecommunications generally, aerial navigation is undergoing rapid change. The most significant development is the introduction of satellite navigation. Already in use is the **global positioning system (GPS)**, now fitted in many airliners. Hand portable GPS sets are available at modest cost and have found their way into small aircraft, boats and even cars. GPS receivers work by picking up the radio signals from a group of dedicated satellites orbiting the earth. They are potentially able to indicate position in all three dimensions (geographical location and height) to an accuracy of a few metres. Once its reliability is proven there is little doubt that satellite navigation will replace most other systems, perhaps even the trusty ILS, which has served the world of aviation for half a century.

Another recent development is for aircraft to be equipped with a **terrain data base**, which can pictorially display on the pilots' HSIs significant terrain surrounding the aircraft's current location as a cross-check of minimum flight altitude data derived from navigation charts.

7
The Autopilot

The primary function of the autopilot is to relieve the pilot flying (PF) of the physical task of controlling the aircraft, which although not difficult is tiring because of the mental concentration demanded to fly the correct three dimensional flight path and speed to the required degree of accuracy. In other words the autopilot is an essential item rather than a luxury.

Additionally, jet airliners at their normal cruising heights are tricky to fly accurately, mainly because the air is thin and the momentum great. (Remember that true airspeeds are in the range of 400 to 500 knots.) Even small pitch attitude adjustments result in large changes of vertical flight path. It has to be said, and you won't find a pilot who denies it, that autopilots fly more accurately than their human counterparts, especially at cruising heights.

The autopilot controls are housed in the glareshield.

How does it work?
The autopilot works by sending electrical signals to the valves in the flight control actuators. Remember that the actuators move the control surfaces by means of pressurised hydraulic fluid and the valves regulate the flow of fluid. You can see then the autopilot is merely mimicking the

actions of PF, who when manually flying is controlling the actuator valves by mechanical inputs from the control wheel.

How are the autopilot signals generated? Firstly, it has to be told what to do. Using the **mode control panel (MCP)** on the glareshield above the centre instrument panel PF can program the autopilot according to the required flight path. For example, it can be programmed to maintain a constant altitude and heading. Or it can be used to make the aircraft climb or descend, or turn onto a different heading.

The inputs from the MCP are sent to the **flight control computer (FCC)**. The FCC compares the MCP demands against what the aircraft is actually doing at the moment, taking its information from the air data computer (which we met earlier when talking about performance). If the aircraft is doing what the MCP is demanding then there are no signals sent to the actuators and the aircraft will maintain its current flight path. Otherwise the FCC computes the new flight path and sends the appropriate signals to the actuator valves, which in turn move the elevators and ailerons as necessary.

Vertical navigation

In **vertical navigation (VNAV)** mode, the MCP controls can be used in one of two ways. In **speed** mode, the autopilot will climb or descend to the selected height at the speed programmed by PF (usually economy speed). The autopilot is using the elevators to control speed by adjustment of pitch attitude, just as a human pilot would. In **path** mode, the autopilot will use the elevators to hold a programmed vertical flight path, for example maintaining constant altitude in the cruise. Once the flight management computer (FMC) (remember that?) has calculated the optimum descent profile the autopilot VNAV path mode can be used to follow this profile, with the elevators now adjusting pitch attitude to do so. (So if the autopilot is in VNAV path mode, you ask, what is controlling speed? The answer, of course, is engine thrust.)

Lateral navigation

The MCP can be used to turn the aircraft onto the headings required to follow the route track line displayed on the pilots' HSIs. But a better way to achieve the same objective is to engage the autopilot **lateral navigation (LNAV)** mode. Now the autopilot will follow the route without any further input necessary from PF, banking the aircraft onto whichever heading is required. Either way, the autopilot is using the ailerons to control heading.

The coupled approach

If we can use the autopilot to follow programmed vertical (up-and-down) and horizontal (left and right) flight paths, can we make it follow the instrument landing system beams when we want to land? The answer is most definitely yes. This is exactly what PF will do if approaching to land in bad weather (poor visibility or low cloud). To carry out a **coupled approach**, then, PF programs the autopilot to intercept and follow the localiser and glideslope beams. The localiser signals are fed via the FCC to the ailerons and the glideslope signals to the elevators.

The autothrottle

When the aircraft's elevators are controlling flight path we know that engine thrust must be used to control speed. Of course, this is true whether or not the autopilot is in use. To reduce PF's workload further, why not arrange for automatic control of thrust?

The device which does this is the **autothrottle**, which physically moves the thrust levers by means of clutches in the console. Depending on the demands from the MCP, the autothrottle operates in one of two modes. In **thrust** mode the autothrottle sets the levers to give constant thrust, either take-off thrust or climb thrust or, for the descent, idle thrust or manually set thrust. In **speed** mode, the auto-throttle moves the levers to maintain the speed set by PF in the MCP.

Let's see how the autopilot and autothrottle work together. Keep in mind that *at all times one of the two has to control speed*. Let's start in the climb. The autopilot will be in VNAV speed mode. The FMC signals the autothrottle to set climb thrust. As the programmed cruise altitude is reached the autopilot will switch to VNAV path mode, using the elevators to level off at this altitude and then maintain it. When the autopilot changes mode, so does the autothrottle, which now switches to speed mode. If the aircraft starts to fly faster or slower than the programmed speed the autothrottle will adjust the thrust levers to correct the error.

At the start of descent point the autothrottle will bring the thrust levers back to idle and the autopilot will now use the elevators to lower the aircraft's nose so that it flies the programmed descent path. But hang on a minute, you say. What is controlling speed if the autopilot is in path mode and the engines are at idle thrust? Well, if the FMC calculated the descent path correctly, the speed should stabilise at the programmed setting with the aircraft in this configuration. And suppose it doesn't? Suppose the speed drops below what is required. In this case the autothrottle will respond by increasing thrust until the speed has been recovered. And if the speed is too high? In this case PF has the choice of allowing surplus speed to build up or else using the speed-brake lever to slow down.

The autothrottle would also be used during a coupled approach when the autopilot is following the ILS. The autothrottle, of course, will be operating in ... can you work out which mode?

When the automatics (autopilot and autothrottle) are making small changes, such as during the cruise, it is not necessary for PF to have his or her hands on the controls. But if large changes are needed, such as when the aircraft starts or finishes a climb or descent, it is good practice for PF to follow through to monitor that the automatics are behaving as they should. This is especially true during the coupled approach when the automatics are being entrusted to fly the aircraft ever closer to the ground, even more so in bad weather.

(The answer to the question above is: **speed** mode.)

The real world

So far we've been carrying on as if we can climb and descend as we please. In reality this is a rare scenario. In busy regions of airspace flights will be forced to fly at speeds and heights dictated by air traffic control, who have to keep all aircraft safely separated from each other. There is a high level of mutual understanding here. The controllers know that pilots like to keep as close as possible to their ideal flight profiles and do their best to accommodate them. By the same token, pilots are aware of how difficult the controllers' job can be, particularly when the sky is busy and or aircraft need to avoid bad weather, such as thunderstorms. They will do whatever the controllers ask of them as long as the aircraft is safely capable of doing it and you will never hear a pilot complaining about being forced to fly off his or her preferred profile.

How would we use the automatics if we found ourselves in this situation? The climb and cruise are not major problems. It is merely a case of patiently waiting until traffic conditions enable the controller to clear us to cruise at our desired height. (We will consume more fuel, of course, if we are obliged to fly below optimum for a long time.) What about the descent? Suppose we are forced down early. Or suppose ATC won't let us descend when we want to. Either of these situations mean that we will have to abandon the ideal descent path, at least for a while. In other words, VNAV path mode won't be available. Instead, we can use the autopilot in VNAV speed mode and autothrottle (thrust mode, manually set) or speedbrake to control descent gradient, depending on whether we're too low or too high. The FMC will tell us how far above or below the ideal path we are. If by good fortune our air traffic control clearance allows us to intercept the ideal path then we can re-engage VNAV path mode, whereupon the autothrottle will revert to either idle thrust or speed mode. Remember, in the descent the aircraft is in its **clean** configuration (flaps up and landing gear retracted). On the approach the flaps and gear are extended and engine thrust is needed to counteract the increased drag.

Figure 26 summarises control of vertical flight path and speed. Of course, it is valid for both automatic and manual aircraft control.

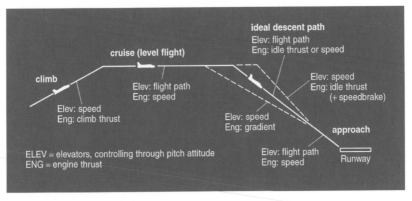

Fig. 26. Control of vertical flight path and speed.

Autoland

If we flew a coupled approach, we would at some stage have to disengage the autopilot and autothrottle and take over manually for landing, otherwise the aircraft would fly into the ground.

If the aircraft has automatic landing capability, however, then there is no need to disengage the automatics. We can let the aircraft **autoland**. To be able to do this, extra equipment is required, such as the radio altimeter. The **radio altimeter** works by sending radio signals vertically down and then timing how long it takes the signals to be reflected back from the ground to the aircraft. The time taken is converted into distance, the radio altimeter being calibrated in feet. Compare this to the conventional altimeter readings on the pilots' display panels, which are derived from measurement of air pressure. The radio altimeter therefore gives an instantaneous readout of height above the terrain immediately below the aircraft.

As we approach the runway, then, the autopilot mimics the action of a human pilot. When the radio altimeter senses that the aircraft has descended to flare height, it takes control of the elevators through the autopilot, which now disregards the glideslope indications. In other words, the autopilot flares for landing just as a human pilot would. At the same time the autothrottle retards the thrust levers to idle.

After touchdown the autopilot uses the elevators to fly the nosewheel onto the runway. The autopilot also switches the localiser signals from the aileron actuators to the rudder actuators. Any tendency of the aircraft to stray from the centre line is thus prevented by opposing rudder inputs. The only action required from PF, apart from following the autopilot and autothrottle movements, is to apply reverse thrust after touchdown (and wheelbraking by foot if the automatic system is not being used).

If we are to entrust our lives to this equipment, we need to be certain of its operational integrity. For this reason it is usual for the aircraft to be fitted with three independent autopilots, each with its own radio altimeter. During the approach to land the three autopilots compare the inputs they are sending to the actuators. If they are all in agreement then the aircraft is allowed to autoland. If one disagrees from the other two it is isolated from the controls and an alert message is sent to the pilots. Depending on circumstances, they may allow the autoland to continue, using the two remaining autopilots. If all three disagree, the alert message will inform the pilots that the aircraft is not capable of completing an automatic landing.

The weather is a big factor here. Later on we'll examine the legal restrictions that bad weather conditions impose on airline operators. For the moment we'll just note that with all the autoland equipment working normally it is permissible to land in very low visibilities, typically less than 100 metres, which is very thick fog. No human pilot could safely land an airliner in these conditions.

You can see that autoland capability is only possible at airports equipped with ILS. Even then, the ILS beams must meet certain precision criteria before aircraft are allowed to autoland there. Most British airports are thus equipped, which means that weather diversions for aircraft with autoland are now a rare occurrence.

The flight director

We saw above how the autopilot worked by sending electrical signals from the flight control computer to the valves in the aileron and elevator actuators. Since the autopilot knows what pitch and bank attitude it should be using, could this information be given to the pilots to help them if they are flying manually? In other words, can the FCC tell the pilots what pitch and bank attitudes to fly?

The answer is yes, and the device that does it is the **flight director**. The FCC commands are presented to the pilots on their attitude indicators in the form of two bars in the shape of a cross.

The **pitch bar** is parallel to the top of the glareshield. It moves up and down and, as its name suggests, indicates the pitch attitude which should be flown to achieve the vertical flight path or speed programmed from the mode control panel. The **roll bar** is at right angles to the pitch bar and it moves left and right. Its interpretation is different from the pitch bar. If PF is flying the correct bank angle the roll bar lies in the middle of the attitude indicator display. If the bar lies to the left, PF must make a roll input to the left until the bar is centred again, at which

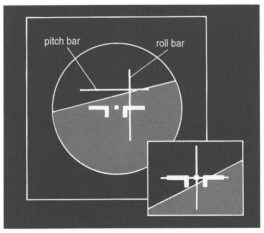

Fig. 27. The flight director. The inset shows the flight director commands satisfied.

The FCC commands are presented to the pilots on their attitude indicators in the form of two bars in the shape of a cross.

The **pitch bar** is parallel to the top of the glareshield. It moves up and down and, as its name suggests, indicates the pitch attitude which should be flown to achieve the vertical flight path or speed programmed from the mode control panel. The **roll bar** is at right angles to the pitch bar and it moves left and right. Its interpretation is different from the pitch bar. If PF is flying the correct bank angle the roll bar lies in the middle of the attitude indicator display. If the bar lies to the left, PF must make a roll input to the left until the bar is centred again, at which point he or she should centre the control wheel because the correct bank angle has been achieved. If the roll bar is displaced to the right the same technique is used to bring it back to the centre. This case could arise, for example, when the MCP controls are used to start a turn to the right, or indeed to finish a left turn. In the example shown the pilot should raise the nose and bank right (increasing the bank angle) to obey the flight director.

Pilots often like to fly manual approaches because it helps to maintain their basic aircraft handling skills. With the MCP programmed to fly an ILS approach the flight director will give the correct pitch and roll commands to help PF maintain the correct profile. It is much easier to fly an accurate ILS approach with the flight director in use than without it.

Is it on autopilot?

This question is frequently asked by flight deck visitors, as is: How much of the flight is done on autopilot? The answer to the second ques-

descent or approach so that the last part of the flight and the landing can be flown manually.

If the weather is not so good or the airspace is busy the pilots tend to make more use of the autopilot, because manual flight on instruments (in other words, without visual reference) demands much more concentration than visual flight. By letting the autopilot do the work the pilots are free to monitor its performance while they carry out their other in-flight duties. The same consideration applies when the human pilots are tired: autopilots never get tired. However, they cannot think for themselves and will do only what they are programmed to do by the human pilots.

Visitors to the flight deck often remark that the pilots don't seem to have much to do, particularly when they are told that the autopilot is flying the aircraft. The scene might indeed appear to be one of inactivity, but the irony is that the visitors have been allowed into the flight deck because at that moment the pilots' workload is low. As you can judge from what you now know, during the take-off and climb and during the descent, approach and landing there is a lot more going on.

Even in the cruise there are duties to be performed. Besides maintaining communication with air traffic control, the pilots must obtain weather reports for en route airports in case the need suddenly arises for an expeditious landing. They must monitor autopilot and autothrottle performance, carry out navigation and fuel checks and they must plan their approach and landing. If the destination airport is surrounded by high terrain, and or the weather is bad, and or the airport is not equipped with ILS, this briefing exercise is done in some detail, as you would expect. And don't forget that although the passengers are deplaning at the destination airport the pilots might not be, in which case they must also start planning for the next departure. They must check the weather at the destination airport and at their alternate airports in case the flight has to be diverted. If you add occasional problems such as storms or turbulence, unexpected rerouting, equipment unserviceabilities and passengers taken ill you can understand why there is often much more flight deck activity than the casual visitor sees. And you can see why the answer to the question which forms the title of this paragraph is always: yes.

8
The Rules of the Air

One reason for the high level of safety that the air transport industry has achieved is the extensive regulation under which the industry operates. It is clear that in regions of sky busy with airliners flying at great speed in various directions and altitudes, not to mention climbing and descending, a sophisticated air traffic control (ATC) regime is essential. Of equal self evidence is the importance of ensuring that there is in place a suitable set of rules governing flight operations, that all operators are aware of the rules and that all operators obey them. Related to these requirements is that of making certain that those personnel directly concerned with aircraft operations are adequately trained and, where necessary, are obliged to prove their knowledge and abilities by means of assessment.

Airspace division

Not surprisingly, it would be impossible for aviation to adopt an equivalent of the 'open seas' policy applying to the maritime industry, where ships' captains can go pretty well where they please once away from port. Instead, the rules of the air are formulated to allow as much freedom in particular regions of airspace as traffic conditions will permit.

To implement the rules, the world's airspace is divided up into areas, each under control of a separate authority. Each area is called a **Flight Information Region (FIR)** or **Control Area (CTA)**, usually named after its geographic location. For example the sky over Britain is divided into the London FIR, covering England and the surrounding seas and the Scottish FIR, covering Scotland, Northern Ireland and the surrounding seas. By contrast the north Atlantic is divided into the Shanwick Oceanic CTA, controlling the airspace of the eastern half (up to longitude 30° west) and the Gander Oceanic CTA, controlling the western half. These names derive from their respective ATC authorities, Shanwick (from Shannon in Ireland and Prestwick in Scotland) and Gander (in Newfoundland).

Within the FIRs there are further airspace divisions. Some regions of sky are reserved primarily for commercial airliner traffic. Many regions of this **controlled airspace** are in the form of corridors. These are the airways, often marked out by radio beacons, which we have already met. Others are areas sited around the main airports. Some airspace is reserved for the exclusive use of the military and some again is prohibited to all traffic for one reason or another.

Separation of traffic

For any aircraft, large or small, to arrive safely at its destination it must obviously avoid other traffic on the way. Outside controlled airspace, when the weather is amenable, pilots themselves are responsible for achieving separation from other aircraft. This is the time honoured 'see-and-be-seen' principle. One of the first things that student pilots learn is to keep a continual lookout for other traffic. If there appears to be conflict the rules of the air dictate the actions that the pilots should take to resolve it. This system, called **visual flight rules (VFR)**, works very well for light aircraft, flying at relatively slow speeds, when the visibility is good and the aircraft can be kept away from cloud.

But of course good weather is an uncertain entity in many parts of the world, particularly Britain and western Europe. If the visibility is poor or the cloud extensive visual traffic separation is impossible. Pilots flying in this sort of weather, even outside controlled airspace, must follow different rules to guarantee separation. The responsibility for separation now falls to air traffic control. The pilots for their part must be qualified for instrument flight (in other words, without visual reference) and must comply with the instructions passed to them by ATC. This procedure is called **instrument flight rules (IFR)**.

Inside controlled airspace the rules are even more restrictive, as you would expect. Airliners must be able to fly their scheduled routes and timetables regardless of weather conditions. Additionally, the see-and-be-seen principle of traffic separation is unworkable for large, relatively unmanoeuvrable aircraft travelling at speeds of more than 500 miles per hour. To be allowed to fly in controlled airspace, then, aircraft must have the capability to be able to navigate without visual reference and the pilots must be qualified in instrument flight. They must comply with ATC instructions, or **clearances**, regardless of the weather conditions. In other words, in controlled airspace aircraft must always fly under IFR, even in good weather. ATC will therefore have full control of all aircraft under their jurisdiction and will know that the pilots are qualified to comply with their clearances. Again, responsibility for traffic separation rests entirely with ATC.

Radar and transponders

Just contrast, for a moment, the scenario of a light aircraft flying outside controlled airspace in good weather against that of an airliner flying in controlled airspace in bad weather. The light aircraft pilot will be continually watching for other traffic and may even be navigating visually as well. As long as he keeps out of controlled and prohibited airspace he can fly where he chooses at whatever altitude he chooses. Only when he approaches his destination airfield do further restrictions apply, concerning the flight path he flies when coming in to land. At airfields without ATC he can even land or take-off without needing anyone's permission.

The airliner crew, on the other hand, will be following their ATC clearance, which specifies the route they must follow and the altitude at which they must fly. When it is time to descend they will be cleared to successively lower altitudes, traffic permitting, as they approach their destination airport. The only time they will need visual reference will be to complete the landing manoeuvre, not even then if they are planning an autoland.

So how do ATC know where all the aircraft in their airspace are? They do it by using **radar** equipment and data links. Radar (radio detection and ranging) works by sending radio signal pulses into the sky. The pulses are reflected back by aircraft in the vicinity and the equipment shows the direction and distance from which the pulses come, each aircraft sending back its own reflected signal.

The air traffic controller can see where the aircraft are by looking at his or her **radarscope**, which resembles a television monitor. Each aircraft shows as a blob of light. Also marked on the screen are the boundaries of controlled airspace and ground features such as airports. How does the controller know which blob corresponds to which aircraft? The data link will do this job. One of the instrument flight rules in controlled airspace is that the aircraft must be fitted with a **transponder**. This device sends coded radio signals to the ATC radar receiver, giving the aircraft's identification letters or flight number and also its altitude (via a signal from the air data computer). By this means the controller has a full three dimensional picture of all the traffic under his or her jurisdiction.

How far away is that other plane?

In controlled airspace each aircraft has its own surrounding envelope of sky, into which no other traffic may intrude. In other words aircraft must be separated by ATC either vertically or horizontally. Under radar control, typical minimum horizontal distances are 3 miles laterally (side by side) and 5 miles longitudinally (ahead and behind) for aircraft flying in the same direction at the same altitude. These minimum distances increase at higher altitudes, where faster true airspeeds make aircraft less manoeuvrable. When necessary ATC will impose speed adjustments to ensure longitudinal separation. If aircraft are closer than the horizontal minimum allowed then they must be separated vertically. Aircraft travelling in different directions must also be separated horizontally or vertically. Minimum vertical separation is 1,000 feet.

Below 10,000 feet there is a universal speed restriction of 250 knots indicated airspeed to make the task of separation easier near airports, where traffic density is naturally greater, although ATC might waive this restriction if traffic is light.

Occasionally ATC take responsibility for navigation by means of radar **vectors**, which are instructions to pilots to fly specified headings. Vectors are often used to maintain adequate lateral separation, or to sequence arriving flights onto the ILS approach. In the first case the pilots will be released to their own navigation again once adequate separation has been achieved. In the second, navigational responsibility reverts to the pilots once they have intercepted the ILS localiser.

In non-radar controlled airspace (such as over oceans and unpopulated areas) the minimum horizontal distances are increased considerably. For example, over the north Atlantic minimum lateral separation is 60 miles and minimum longitudinal separation ten minutes. For this reason the ATC clearance will also specify cruise Mach number as well as route. Pilots of aircraft flying in non-radar controlled airspace are obliged to make regular position reports so that ATC can be sure that adequate separation is being maintained.

A recent addition to airliner flight decks is the **traffic alert and collision avoidance system (TCAS)**. This works by processing the signals from the transponders of other aircraft in the vicinity. On the pilots' horizontal situation indicators the TCAS computer displays the relative position of other traffic and the altitude it is flying at. If it senses that a conflict has arisen it alerts the pilots and gives the recommended avoidance action. The TCAS system is intended as a back up to normal ATC, not a replacement for it.

Altimeter setting

Remember that the altimeter works by sensing air pressure around the aircraft. As we go higher the air pressure reduces and the altimeter converts the pressure reading into an indication of altitude. But there is a snag here, because air pressure also depends on the weather (which is how a barometer works) and an altimeter cannot tell the difference between low pressure resulting from greater altitude or that resulting from weather.

The answer to the problem is to make the altimeter settable to a given datum. For take-off and landing the datum is sea level pressure at the airport, stated in millibars (or hectopascals, which are the same thing). This datum is given the code form **QNH**. The altimeter of an aircraft sitting on the ground, set to QNH, will indicate the **elevation** of the airport (that is, its height above sea level). The QNH setting is clearly vital when flying near the ground in cloud, because the pilots will be using their altimeters to make sure that the aircraft never descends below the minimum flight altitude shown on their navigation charts. (What about the radio altimeter, you say. Won't that show you your height above the ground? Yes, it will, and pilots do indeed monitor their radio altimeters when close to the ground. But remember that this instrument shows only vertical clearance immediately beneath the aircraft. It could not detect the presence of high terrain just in front of the aircraft.)

We have already found out that ATC separates traffic vertically by allocating different altitudes to different aircraft. An airliner flying along an airway in one direction might be cleared to fly at 37,000 feet, and one in the opposite direction at 38,000 feet, giving the standard separation. But suppose that one of these aircraft took-off from an airport situated in an area of high air pressure (high QNH set on its altimeter) and then flew towards a region of lower pressure. The altimeter would interpret the lower pressure as gain in altitude and the pilot (or autopilot) would need to descend to achieve the original indication on the altimeter. Conversely, an aircraft that departed from a region of low air pressure (low QNH) towards a region of higher pressure would have to climb to maintain a constant altimeter indication. When these two aircraft passed in flight it could mean that the actual separation between them might be more than 1,000 feet. More worryingly, it might be less. The obvious solution is to require all aircraft in controlled airspace to set a standard altimeter setting once they have taken off and to use this setting until approaching to land. This standard setting is 1,013 millibars (or hectopascals). The indication on the altimeters is divided by a factor of 100 and is now called the **flight level (FL)**. So with their altimeters set to 1,013 the two aircraft mentioned above are flying at FL 370 and FL 380 respectively, and the separation between them is exactly 1,000 feet.

To summarise altimeter setting and terminology:
* the word 'height' implies vertical distance above a specified datum. If the datum is an airport then the height of an aircraft on the ground is zero.
* if the datum is sea level then the word 'altitude' replaces 'height'. For example, Birmingham airport has an elevation of 300 feet (in other words the airport is 300 feet above sea level). Let us say that an aircraft is flying over the airport with its altimeter set to Birmingham QNH. If the altimeter reads, say, 2,000 feet, then the aircraft's **altitude** is 2,000 feet but its **height** is 1,700 feet.
* the words 'flight level' refer to the altimeter indication, divided by 100, when the altimeter is set to 1,013 millibars or hectopascals.

In future, it might come about that altimetry is based on GPS signals rather than measurement of air pressure. Aircraft altitudes could then be referenced to a sea level datum, obviating the need for altimeter resetting during the various phases of flight and thereby removing a potential source of human error.

9
Radio Communications

One of the freedoms for the light-aircraft pilot flying under visual flight rules outside controlled airspace is that there is no obligation to use the radio. Indeed many such aircraft are not even fitted with radio equipment. But clearly commercial aviation activity would be impossible without communication between air traffic control and pilots.

Additionally, pilots use their radios to talk to their operations staff, to other aircraft if necessary and to listen to weather broadcasts transmitted for this purpose.

Radio communication differs from telephone conversation in that several aircraft may be using the same frequency if they are talking to the same air traffic controller in a particular region of airspace. For this reason, aircraft must identify themselves when they transmit a message so that the controller knows which one the message has come from. To achieve this, every aircraft must have an individual **callsign**. Additionally, standard words and phrases are used whenever possible to facilitate rapid and unambiguous communication. The language to be used is either English or the national language in the region of airspace concerned. Use of standard words and phrases makes communication easier for pilots and controllers whose first language is not English. If words or phrases need to be spelt out, the **phonetic alphabet** (Fig. 28) is used:

By monitoring the radio transmissions from other aircraft on the same frequency, pilots can build up a mental picture of the traffic in their proximity, thereby checking that adequate separation is being maintained by ATC.

Fig. 28. Phonetic alphabet

A	Alpha	N	November
B	Bravo	O	Oscar
C	Charlie	P	Papa
D	Delta	Q	Quebec
E	Echo	R	Romeo
F	Foxtrot	S	Sierra
G	Golf	T	Tango
H	Hotel	U	Uniform
I	India	V	Victor
J	Juliet	W	Whiskey
K	Kilo	X	X-ray
L	Lima	Y	Yankee
M	Mike	Z	Zulu

To illustrate how controllers speak to the aircraft under their control, and vice versa, let us follow the progress of Interflight 547 from Birmingham, England to Las Palmas, Gran Canaria. We'll listen in as it prepares to depart from its gate. The pilots are talking to the Ground Control. PNF will make the transmissions from the aircraft.

Ground: 'Interflight 547, I have your ATC clearance.'

PNF: 'Interflight 547, ready to copy.'

Ground: 'Interflight 547, cleared to Golf Charlie Lima Papa, Compton Two Delta departure, squawk six two five six.'

PNF: 'Interflight 547, cleared to Golf Charlie Lima Papa, Compton Two Delta departure, squawk six five two six.'

Ground: 'Interflight 547, the squawk is 6256.'

PNF: 'Interflight 547, squawk 6256.'

Ground: 'Interflight 547, read back correct.'

The phrase 'Golf Charlie Lima Papa' is the code for Las Palmas airport, GCLP. 'Compton 2D departure' defines the initial routing after take-off towards Compton, which is a radio beacon situated a few miles to the west of Reading in Berkshire. This departure allows the aircraft

The highest location at the airport: the control tower.

to climb initially to Flight Level 60 (6,000 feet with the altimeter set to 1,013 millibars). Since no further route instructions have been notified, the implication is that Interflight 547 can follow the route submitted to air traffic control by the Interflight Airlines operations staff.

The 'squawk' of 6256 is the code to be set on the aircraft's transponder. Initially PNF repeated the wrong code and so the ground controller had to correct him. This 'reading back' of important information is the guarantee that both ATC and pilots are in agreement about the clearance.

Later on Interflight 547 is taxiing towards the holding point for runway 33. The holding point is on the taxiway just short of the runway threshold.

Ground: 'Interflight 547 contact Tower, one one eight decimal three, goodbye.'

PNF: 'Interflight 547 contact one one eight three, goodbye.'

PNF will now change the frequency on the aircraft's VHF radio to 118.3 Megahertz so that they can talk to the control tower.

PNF: 'Birmingham Tower, Interflight 547, good morning, ready for departure.'

Tower: 'Good morning, Interflight 547, line up runway three three.'

Climbing away from Lyons airport in Southern France.

PNF: 'Cleared to line up, Interflight 547.'

And as they are lining up:
Tower: 'Interflight 547 cleared take-off runway three three,
                        wind two eight zero, twelve.'
PNF: 'Cleared take-off, Interflight 547.'

When Tower cleared the aircraft for take-off, the controller also gave the
surface wind, which was blowing from direction 280° (magnetic) at 12
knots. Since runway 33 by definition points approximately in the direction 330° magnetic, the aircraft will have a headwind component for this
take-off, and also a crosswind from the left.

   After take-off, tower will hand over Interflight 547 to Birmingham
radar, which controls the airspace round the airport, who will in turn
transfer it to London Control. We'll join the flight a few minutes later.
London: 'Interflight 547, climb flight level two six zero, con-
                        tact one three five decimal three two.'
PNF: 'Interflight 547 climb level two six zero, one three
                        five three two.'

Having selected the new frequency on the VHF radio:
PNF: 'London, Interflight 547, good morning, climbing
                        flight level two six zero.'
London: 'Good morning, Interflight 547, turn left heading
                        one seven five, climb flight level two eight zero.'
PNF: 'Left one seven five, climb level two eight zero,
                        Interflight 547.'

The aircraft is still in the London FIR, but the density of traffic means
that the sky must be divided into relatively small sectors, which is why
Interflight 547 is now talking to a different London controller. This
controller has given the aircraft a vector, in other words a heading to fly,
probably to facilitate traffic separation.

A little later:
London: 'Interflight 547, own navigation direct Ortac, say
                        level requested.'
PNF: 'Direct Ortac, requesting flight level three six zero,
                        Interflight 547.'
London: 'Interflight 547 climb flight level three three zero,
                        final level in London, request higher from Brest.'
PNF: 'Climb level three three zero, Interflight 547.'

Responsibility for navigation has passed back to the pilots, who must
now reprogramme the flight management computer to take the aircraft

direct to Ortac, which is a waypoint over the Channel on the boundary between British and French airspace. Besides being included in the FMC data base, Ortac will also be shown on the pilots' aeronautical charts. The ATC clearance direct to Ortac implies that the intervening beacons and waypoints can be bypassed. The crew of Interflight 547 want to cruise at 36,000 feet, which is probably as close to the optimum as they can get. London has cleared Interflight 547 up to FL 330, perhaps because other traffic is occupying higher levels. The controller is suggesting that they might get clearance to fly higher later in the flight when they are under Brest control.

As the aircraft approaches Ortac:

London: 'Interflight 547, maintain level three three zero, contact Brest Control on one three four decimal eight two, goodbye.'

PNF: 'Interflight 547 to one three four decimal eight two, goodbye.'

Having selected the new frequency:

PNF: 'Brest, good morning, Interflight 547 level three three zero, requesting three six zero.'

Brest: 'Bonjour, Interflight 547, maintain level three three zero, expect higher, proceed Quimper Lotee.'

PNF: 'Interflight 547 maintaining level three three zero, proceeding Quimper Lotee.'

Quimper is a radio beacon on the west coast of the Britanny peninsular and Lotee a waypoint over the Bay of Biscay where French airspace joins Spanish airspace. There will be a few more frequency changes as Interflight 547 crosses the various sectors in French airspace. Let us suppose that the aircraft has been cleared to climb to FL 360. At Lotee, Brest Control will hand the flight over to Madrid Control:

Brest: 'Interflight 547, contact Madrid one three five seven, au revoir.'

PNF: 'One three five decimal seven, Interflight 547, goodbye.'

On the new frequency:

PNF: 'Madrid, Interflight 547 level three six zero, good morning.'

Madrid: 'Buenos dias, Interflight 547. Maintain three six zero on course Alpha Victor Sierra.'

PNF: 'To Asturias, Interflight 547.'

In this exchange the Madrid controller has spelt out phonetically the identification code for the radio beacon at Asturias, on the northern Spanish coast. This particular beacon transmits the letters 'AVS' in Morse code so that anyone using it for navigation can confirm that they are tuned to the right frequency. After a brief transit through Spanish airspace Interflight 547 will be transferred to Lisbon Control as they enter Portuguese airspace.

The planned route goes down the length of Portugal and then leaves Europe behind as it crosses the coast just south of Lisbon. From now on the aircraft will by flying over the eastern Atlantic Ocean, its route roughly paralleling the Moroccan coastline, about 200 miles out to sea. The boundary between Portuguese and Moroccan airspace lies about 150 miles south of Lisbon, at which point control of Interflight 547 will be handed over to Casablanca control.

Interflight 547 will arrive at the boundary with Canaries airspace about 200 miles northeast of Gran Canaria. On handover the crew will be given the expected arrival routing. Soon the aircraft is nearing the point where the flight management computer recommends starting down. Of course, permission is required:

PNF: 'Canarias, Interflight 547 request descent.'

Canarias: 'Interflight 547 stand by, break, Air Britain 123 Bravo maintain level three nine zero, contact Casablanca one two four decimal five.'

Air Britain 123 B: 'Casa on one two four five, Air Britain 123 Bravo, adios.'

Canarias: 'Interflight 547 cleared descend flight level one five zero.'

PNF: 'Interflight 547 cleared level one five zero, leaving three six zero.'

In this exchange, Canarias Control had an important message to transmit to Air Britain 123 B and so Interflight 547 was told to wait. The word 'break' means another aircraft is going to be addressed.

As it approaches Las Palmas airport Interflight 547 will be handed over to approach control, who will vector it onto the ILS. It's a nice day and the pilots can see the airport clearly. Runway 03L is in use (what direction does that point in?) and the controller's heading is positioning them over the sea to the east of the airport. The runway is visible on the right hand side as the aircraft flies parallel to it in the opposite direction. PF asks PNF to transmit a request for permission to make a visual approach, flying a right hand circuit pattern, which will be more expeditious. Here's the exchange:

PNF: 'Las Palmas, Interflight 547, runway in sight, request visual approach.'

Approach: 'Negative, Interflight 547, you are number two, maintain heading two one zero, descend altitude

	two thousand feet, QNH one zero one eight.'
PNF:	'Descend altitude two thousand feet, QNH one zero one eight, maintain heading, Interflight 547.'

The Approach controller cannot agree to the pilots' request because there is another aircraft already making an approach. Clearing Interflight 547 for a visual approach might infringe minimum separation requirements. The pilots will not argue with this although if they can see the first aircraft they might make the request again, accepting responsibility for maintaining adequate separation themselves. Today the conflicting traffic is approaching from another direction and the pilots of Interflight 547 cannot yet see it. The controller vectors them towards the localiser:

Approach:	'Interflight 547 turn right heading three six zero, cleared to intercept localiser.'

FNP acknowledges and PF (either manually or through the autopilot) flies heading 360° until intercepting the localiser, now turning further right to follow it.

PNF:	'Interflight 547 established localiser.'
Approach:	'Interflight 547 cleared ILS approach, contact tower on one one eight three.'

Fig. 29. Approach to Las Palmas airport.

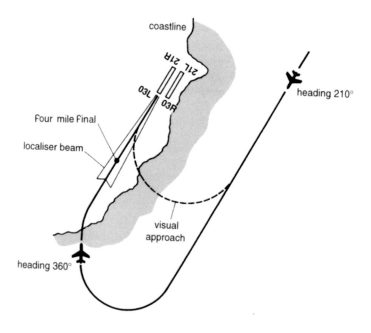

PNF selects Tower frequency.

PNF:	'Tower, Interflight 547, established localiser.'
Tower:	'Buenos dias Interflight 547, call four mile final.'

PF maintains 2,000 feet until the glideslope beam comes in and then follows it down. The controller possibly has an aircraft waiting to take-off on runway 03L, or perhaps the preceding arriving flight has not yet landed and Interflight 547's call at four miles from touchdown on final approach will help him to sequence his departures and arrivals.

PNF:	'Interflight 547 four mile final.'
Tower:	'Interflight 547 cleared to land runway zero three left, wind zero four zero, one five.'
PNF:	'Cleared land runway zero three left, Interflight 547.'

Having landed and cleared the runway (did they have a headwind or tailwind? Was there a crosswind?) Tower will hand the aircraft to ground control for parking instructions.

10
Meteorology

It is self evident that the weather is of vital importance to all aviation activity. Besides obvious phenomena such as wind, cloud and fog, we have already seen that factors such as air temperature and pressure are also of relevance because of their effect on aircraft performance. Let's start by expanding our knowledge of the properties of the atmosphere.

Atmospheric properties

The temperature of the air closest to the earth's surface is related to the temperature of the surface itself. So the air in the polar regions is colder than in the tropics, although it is not the sun itself which heats the air,

Descending to FL80 above a bank of cumulus cloud, this 757 is approaching the VOR beacon at Pollensa in Mallorca, for an eventual landing on runway 24R at Palma airport.

but contact with the land or sea. At night time the surface gets cooler, but land cools down much more quickly than the sea. Any cloud in the sky has the effect of screening the sun's heat in the daytime and trapping the heat at night. In a cloudless desert, then, air temperature can be very hot during the day and very cold at night. At sea, if the skies are cloudy, there may be hardly any change at all. As we know, air temperature reduces as we climb higher in the atmosphere, at the rate of about 2°C for every 1,000 feet.

When the air is heated by the earth's surface it gets lighter and starts to rise. This movement is called **convection**. In adjacent locations descending air sinks to the surface to replace the rising air. Updraughts and downdraughts encountered by aircraft in flight are often the result of atmospheric convection.

Atmospheric pressure at sea level varies from about 950 millibars (or hectopascals) to about 1,050 millibars. On a weather chart air pressure is shown in the form of **isobars**, which are lines joining locations experiencing the same sea level air pressure. Like temperature, air pressure also reduces as we climb higher in the atmosphere, which is of course how the altimeter works and also why the difference between true airspeed and indicated airspeed increases. (Can you remember how the airspeed indicator works?)

Fig. 30. Weather chart with isobars and fronts.

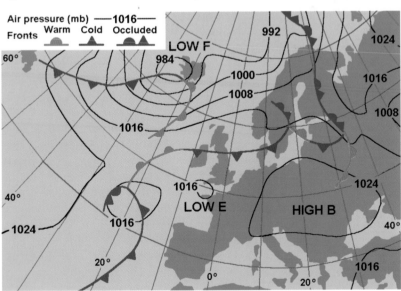

Two other properties related to weather phenomena are **humidity** and **stability**. The former refers to the amount of water vapour in the air, dry air holding very little and humid air holding more. Hot air can hold more vapour than cold air, but only until it is **saturated**, which means that it can take no more. So what happens if we take some saturated air and then cool it? The answer is that some of the vapour condenses out as water droplets. The temperature at which this happens is called the **dew point**. To assess the humidity of a sample of air, then, all we need do is compare its temperature to its dew point. If there is a big difference the air is dry, if not it is humid. And if the temperature equals the dew point the air is obviously saturated.

We have already looked at vertical motion of the air when we considered thermal convection. Once the lifting has occurred, will the air go on rising? That depends on its stability. If it is stable the air will settle again when the lifting influence is removed. If not it will go on rising of its own accord. Any updraughts and downdraughts will be more pronounced in unstable air and the occupants of aircraft can expect a rougher ride. Humid air is less stable than dry air. We shall see the importance of this fact later.

Wind

Air in a region of high pressure (called an **anticyclone**) will naturally try to flow to low pressure regions (**depressions**), which is how winds occur. But the motion of the air is not direct – it is affected by the earth's rotation. Thus the flow of air into a depression takes the form of a spiral, with the wind flowing along the isobars rather than across them. North of the equator the spiral is always counter-clockwise, and the flow out from an anticyclone is always clockwise. In the southern hemisphere these directions are reversed.

When the isobars are close together there is a steep pressure gradient and the winds will be strong. A shallow pressure gradient, indicated on a weather chart by spaced out isobars, will be characterised by light winds.

Clearly the wind direction (by which we mean the direction *from which* it blows) depends on the relative locations of anticyclones and depressions. In many regions of the world, however, the surface winds tend to come from one general direction. In Britain, for example, the *prevailing* winds tend to be from the west and southwest, which is why most runways are aligned in this direction. (Notable exceptions are Birmingham, Cardiff and Leeds-Bradford, where pilots are therefore more likely to encounter crosswinds during take-off and landing.) By contrast, in equatorial regions winds tend to come from the northeast (north of the equator) and southeast (south of the equator.) Some of the world's prevailing winds are still called **trade winds**, reflecting their importance during the era of sailing ships. Topography also affects the direction of surface winds. For example a wind will try to flow along rather across a valley.

Surface winds are usually less than thirty knots in strength. Above this speed they are referred to as **gales** or **severe gales**, and stronger still as **hurricanes** (or **cyclones** or **typhoons** in other areas of the world). Hurricanes are areas of intense low air-pressure. Because of the spiral airflow pattern they are sometimes called tropical revolving storms. Wind speeds in excess of 150 knots (170 mph) have been recorded. Fortunately, hurricanes are rare at latitudes outside the band 30° north to 30° south of the equator.

Strong winds can make life difficult for pilots. At low level, features such as hills and mountains, and even large buildings, can stir the air into turbulent eddies as it flows past. Aircraft control will require greater concentration and the passengers will get a bumpy ride. As we already know, if the wind is across the runway take-off and landing will be trickier. Aircraft manufacturers always specify the maximum permitted crosswind component. Typically this will be 30 to 40 knots. A stronger crosswind will require an arriving flight to be diverted to an airport with a runway more closely aligned with the wind direction.

In the upper atmosphere very strong winds are common. The strongest are called **jetstreams**, and are a benefit or a hindrance to airliners, depending on the direction they are blowing from. An aircraft whose true airspeed is 460 knots (530 mph) with a 100 knot jetstream on its tail will cross the earth's surface at 560 knots (640 mph). If it turns round and flies into the wind its groundspeed will drop to 360 knots (420 mph). Caution is required when flying in or near jet-streams because the very strength of the wind often brings about turbulence.

Visibility

Visibility is expressed in kilometres (km) or, if it is very poor, in metres (m). Droplets of moisture in the atmosphere (cloud, mist and fog) reduce visibility, as do rain, snow and hail. Solid particles (of smoke and dirt) give rise to haze. Pilots of aircraft flying under instrument flight rules (IFR) do not require visual reference of any sort, except to be able to see the runway lights for take-off and the approach and runways lights for landing. If an automatic landing is to be carried out, there must still be enough visual reference for the pilots to be certain that the autopilot is flying the manoeuvre correctly. The exception is when both the on-board aircraft equipment and also the instrument landing system (ILS) installation at the airport meet special precision criteria. In these circumstances autoland is permitted with no requirement for visual reference whatsoever.

Cloud

Whenever air is forced to rise in the atmosphere it cools and so its ability to hold water vapour decreases. If the air continues to rise, then, its humidity increases until it becomes saturated, whereupon the vapour condenses into droplets. In other words, cloud will be formed. Examples of lifting influences are thermal convection and rising terrain over which a wind is blowing.

Cloud can be broadly divided into **stratus** (layer formation) and **cumulus** (heap formation). Stratus cloud is generally uniform in appearance and is associated with stable air. Cumulus cloud has a more irregular appearance, with well defined edges. It is associated with less stable air and therefore its vertical extent tends to be greater. In humid, unstable air cloud can build into towering masses, called **cumulonimbus**, some of which develop into thunderstorms.

At altitudes lower than the **freezing level** the air temperature is greater than 0°C and any cloud consists entirely of water droplets suspended in saturated air. Above the freezing level (where the temperature is less than 0°C) the composition changes to a mixture of ice crystals and supercooled water droplets. The highest cloud is composed almost entirely of ice crystals.

An aircraft flying through cloud higher than the freezing level will encounter these supercooled droplets, which freeze on impact. Thus a layer of ice will build up on the forward facing areas of the aircraft. Although the mass of ice has a negligible effect on aircraft performance, the change in wing contour shape cannot be ignored. Ice on the leading

Developing cumulonimbus cloud.

edges disturbs the normal airflow patterns and so reduces lift and increases drag. Aircraft designed for flight in all weathers, then, must be equipped with anti-icing equipment. For jet airliners this means taking hot air from the engine compressors and sending it through ducts along the leading edges of the wings to melt any ice that would otherwise build up. Other surfaces needing anti-ice protection are the front of the engine cowlings (by hot air, to remove the problems of disrupted airflow and ice ingestion into the engines), the probes measuring air pressure for the air data computer and the angle-of-attack sensors for the stall-warning system. These probes and sensors are heated electrically. The flight deck windscreens also use electrical heating to prevent visual obscurity by ice (outside) or condensation (inside).

Precipitation

In thicker clouds the droplets of water tend to coagulate, brought together by air currents. If they become large enough they will fall as drizzle, or larger still as rain. Above the freezing level some of the ice crystals grow into snowflakes, which may fall to the surface without melting in cold weather. In cumulonimbus cloud water drops carried aloft in the updraughts may freeze suddenly into hailstones, which are often large enough to fall to the earth's surface without melting, even in summer.

Fog

Fog usually forms when night-time skies are cloudless, allowing the land to cool, and hence the air above it. In summer it is unlikely that the air will be cooled to its dew point, but in other seasons the dew point may be reached, in which case condensation will occur in the form of dew and or fog, particularly if the wind is calm or almost so. Fog is also more prevalent in coastal locations, where the air humidity is naturally higher. We already understand the significance of fog to aviation activity. Landing in very low visibilities can only safely be done by automatic systems. Aircraft without autoland capability will have to divert. Fog-bound airports without precision instrument landing system installations will not be able to receive arriving flights, even those equipped with autoland.

Thunderstorms

The hazards arising from thunderstorms are, surprisingly, less to do with electrical activity than with air currents. Lightning strikes on air-craft are not uncommon and rarely do any damage apart from minor burn marks where the electric current enters and leaves the airframe, although the noise of a strike can be disconcerting. Static electricity discharging from the extremities of the airframe can be spectacular in the dark but is not hazardous.

The main reason pilots give thunderstorms as wide a berth as possible is to avoid the turbulence associated with the strong updraughts and downdraughts. Aircraft themselves are designed to be able to withstand severe turbulence, although flight path control will be difficult, even for the autopilot, and the occupants will have a miserable time being thrown around, with the risk of injury if their seat belts are not fastened.

Turbulence in thunderstorms tends to be most severe near areas of heavy precipitation. If pilots flying in cloud could detect these areas they would be able to steer clear of them. The equipment that does this is the **weather radar**. In the nose of the aircraft a transmitter sends out radio signal pulses in the forward direction. The pulses are reflected back by water drops in the cloud and picked up by the receiver, also in the nose. The signals are processed and displayed on the pilots' horizontal situation indicators, colour coded to show intensity. Areas of light precipitation show as green on the HSIs. Heavier intensity is marked in yellow, and heavier still in red. By steering round the yellow and red areas the aircraft will avoid the worst of the turbulence. Severe thunderstorm activity on the approach to the destination airport might mean holding clear until the storm has passed, or even diversion to an alternate airport.

Turbulence

We have seen that turbulence can be generated by unstable air or strong winds or thunderstorms. If it occurs in cloudless skies it is called **clear air turbulence**. This can often be predicted by the meteorologists but it is impossible to detect in flight. If an aircraft unavoidably or unexpectedly encounters severe turbulence the pilots will adjust their speed to the **turbulence penetration speed** specified in the Flight Manual, which minimises airframe stress. For the Boeing 767 this speed is 290 knots indicated or Mach 0.78. The pilots will also consider requesting clearance from air traffic control to descend to a lower cruising altitude if they are close to maximum, to increase the buffet-free speed range (which we looked at in the chapter on performance).

Air masses and fronts

An **air mass** is a region of air having consistent atmospheric properties, these properties reflecting its origin. An air mass arriving over Britain from the Atlantic Ocean will be moist, with greater likelihood of cloud and rain. By contrast, an air mass from continental Europe will be dry, warmer than from the Atlantic in summer, but colder in winter.

At the boundary between two air masses will be a **front**, examples of which are shown in Figure 30. If a warm air mass is displacing a cold one we will find a **warm front** at the boundary. A warm front is heralded by wispy high **cirrus** cloud, which gradually thickens into stratus and lowers as the front approaches. Drizzle will fall, then rain. After the front passes the air temperature increases and the weather improves again. There is often a change in wind direction. A **cold front** marks the boundary where a cold air mass is displacing a warm one. It too is characterised by cloud, but of cumulus type. Precipitation can be heavy and in a marked front there may be thunderstorms. After the front has passed the air temperature will be cooler but the weather will start to improve again, with clearing showers. Again the wind often shifts in direction with the passage of a cold front.

When a warm air mass is lifted clear of the earth's surface by two cold air masses joining together an occlusion (or **occluded front**) occurs, marked by frontal weather characteristics.

Airport operating minima

Suppose an aircraft arrives over the destination airport and the weather isn't too good. Should the pilots attempt a landing? The answer is, of course, that it depends. To start with, what do we mean by bad weather? Poor visibility? Low cloud? Strong crosswind? A combination of these?

And what if the intended runway for landing is not equipped with ILS? How can we navigate in cloud to a point from which a manual landing can be carried out visually? We will have to resort to using radio beacons. The drawback is that guidance from these beacons is not as precise as the ILS and so it would be foolhardy to use them in unsuitable weather. Another alternative (if it is available) is to request guidance from ATC, with the controller giving radar vectors towards the runway and advising the corresponding altitude profile (the so-called 'talk-down' procedure), but again precision falls short of that which the ILS offers.

For these reasons, the aviation authorities define the minimum weather standards which must be met for landing. These **airport operating minima (AOM)** are published by the authorities and no pilot may legally attempt a landing if the minima are not satisfied. For each type of approach, two figures are given, one referring to **decision altitude (DA)** and the other to **runway visual range (RVR)**.

The DA refers to the lowest altitude down to which PF can fly without outside visual reference. (Remember that altitude is height above sea level – the altimeter must be set to QNH.) If at DA the approach lights cannot be clearly seen PF must carry out a go-around manoeuvre, climbing away into the specified missed approach pattern. In other words at DA, PF must decide whether the visual reference is adequate to allow a safe landing to be made. RVR is a measure of horizontal visibility. If the reported actual RVR is less than the minimum permitted the aircraft is not allowed even to attempt an approach.

For an ILS approach, DA usually equates to a height of 200 feet above airport elevation, which should ensure visual contact with the lights in all but the lowest cloud. Typical minimum RVR is 550 metres. Navigation in cloud using other radio beacons or radar talk-down is not as accurate as ILS and so the DA will be higher, as will the minimum RVR requirement.

In very low visibilities, extra procedures apply. The airport ILS installation must meet special precision requirements. Additionally air traffic control must ensure that aircraft on the ground are kept away from the runway area when arriving flights are using the ILS. These **low**

747s of British Airways and Qantas.

visibility procedures (LVPs) ensure that the localiser and glide-slope beams are undistorted, which in turn means that lower AOMs can be used. For approaches in these conditions the radio altimeters are used rather than the pressure altimeters because they are more precise, and so DA is replaced by DH (decision height), in this case height above ground level. Typical minima are DH 50 feet and RVR 200 metres. Manual landing is prohibited, and at DH the task of PF is to confirm by visual reference that the autopilot is flying the correct profile for an automatic landing.

Some aircraft fitted with triple autopilots are permitted to land with no visual reference required whatsoever. The pilots' instruments will tell them when the aircraft has landed (if they cannot feel the touchdown). There is no decision height and the minimum RVR requirement is purely so that PF has enough visual reference to be able to taxi off the runway at the end of the landing roll. Typically this figure is 75 metres, which equates to very thick fog.

Take-off in very low visibilities is an easier manoeuvre to carry out than landing. Automatic take-off is not yet available and so PF will use manual control inputs. For a runway with good lighting, typical minimum RVR is 150 metres.

Weather information

During their pre-flight planning the pilots will study weather information relevant to their intended route. They will be concerned with departure airport conditions (for aircraft performance calculations as well as handling considerations) and the current and forecast conditions at suitable en route airports, destination airport and selected alternates. Alternate airports must be considered in case the flight cannot land at its intended destination, because of bad weather or for other reasons.

Also of relevance are charts showing significant weather that might be encountered during the flight (including cloud, fronts, thunderstorms, icing conditions and turbulence) and forecast wind direction and strength at various altitudes (including jetstreams).

In flight, weather information is obtained by listening to radio broadcasts giving current conditions at airports in the area through which the aircraft is transiting. These broadcasts are continuous and are updated periodically, typically every half hour. As the pilots approach the destination they listen to the **automatic terminal information service (ATIS)** for the airport. The ATIS also broadcasts continuously, with frequent updating of weather and additional relevant information such as which runway is in use for landing.

Many modern airliners are now fitted with satellite based data links and on-board printers. Their pilots can thereby get weather and other pertinent information and have it printed out in the flight deck, which besides being more convenient also obviates the problem of trying to obtain reports by radio in parts of the world where the service is poor or non-existent.

De-icing a 737.

11
Pre-flight Preparation

An important part of the pilots' job, not always recognised by the travelling public, is the preparation that must be done before flight. Most of this preparation is concerned with obtaining data and reviewing its relevance to the planned flight. We have already dealt with one aspect of this when we looked at the importance of meteorological data.

Notams and flight plans

Notam stands for 'notice to airmen'. Notams are published by the national aviation authorities to inform personnel involved in aviation operations of significant factors. Those of concern to pilots deal with items such as unserviceability of radio beacons or changes to published runway dimensions because of construction work, particularly at departure airport, destination airport and alternates, or changes to the published times at which these airports are open. If the operating capacity of an airport has been affected by snowfalls, information is promulgated by **snotams**, dealing with availability of swept runways and taxiways and braking effectiveness on these surfaces. All major airports

Preparing the flight deck.

have briefing units where pilots can obtain weather and notam information. Most of the larger airlines now subscribe to services offering computerised flight planning. By entering their flight number, pilots can call up from the data base weather and notam information pertinent to that flight and also the expected route and fuel requirements.

Air traffic control (ATC) must be formally notified of the flight's details. This is normally done by the airline's operations department, who submit a **flight plan**. ATC may require changes to be made before accepting the flight plan. For example, a different routing might be specified. On busy routes a **slot** might be issued, which is the specific time when the aircraft will be allowed to take-off.

Company instructions and notices

Airline managers publish internal instructions and notices to inform pilots and cabin crew of factors which may be relevant to the airline's operations. Some may be of great significance, such as changes to standard procedures, while others may deal with minor administrative items. It is the responsibility of the pilots to make sure that they are briefed on factors affecting the conduct of flight they are about to undertake.

How much fuel do we need?

The captain of the aircraft must make the decision about how much fuel should be loaded. The legal minimum amount will be enough to fly the aircraft from departure airport to destination (with a 5% contingency allowance), carry out an approach and go-around and divert to a nominated suitable alternate airport, plus enough to hold overhead the alternate for 30 minutes and then land there. The contingency fuel is to cater for such eventualities as re-routing once airborne or less favourable winds than forecast.

Easy, you say, just fill the tanks. But will full tanks be enough? And what about take-off performance? Filling the tanks might make the aircraft too heavy for the prevailing circumstances. And, as always, there are economic factors. The lighter the aircraft at take-off, the less fuel will be needed for the flight. If we carry extra fuel, some of it will be burnt purely to carry it. Typically the penalty is about 4% per hour of flight. If you stick on an extra tonne of fuel, you will burn an extra 40 kilograms for every hour you are in the air. The increased mass also means more wear and tear on the engines, airframe and landing gear.

Carriage of extra fuel might be justified in some circumstances, however. If the forecast weather at destination is poor then increased holding fuel might be sensible in case it is necessary to wait for an improvement. This would also be true if the arrival time coincided with a busy period, with flights turning up at a faster rate than ATC can

Inflight meals for the passengers and crew are being delivered to this 767 by the catering truck on the left.

sequence them on to the approach. In some regions of the world with less sophisticated ATC, pilots might have trouble getting clearance to cruise close to their optimum level, which again means that the fuel burn will be greater. And if fuel is expensive at the destination airport it might be worthwhile economically to carry extra fuel inbound to minimise the subsequent uplift, despite the burn penalty.

If their airline makes use of computerised flight planning, the pilots will be presented with data tailored to their particular flight. The minimum fuel calculation will have been made by the computer taking into account the predicted en route winds. (Headwinds will increase the fuel required and tailwinds will decrease it.) If a computer fuel plan is not available the pilots must use the weather charts to assess the wind component themselves and then refer to tables in the aircraft flight manual to determine the fuel requirement.

The next step is to calculate maximum allowed take-off mass to see whether the required amount of fuel can be lifted. If it cannot it will be necessary to reduce aircraft mass by other means (such as reducing payload) or else plan a refuelling stop en route.

To complete the flight planning described above will typically take half an hour, less for a short flight, more for a long one, especially when the aircraft will be over-flying ocean or desert areas, when contingency plans for en route landing must be considered in greater detail. For ocean crossing it might also be necessary to plot the intended route on special charts printed for this purpose. Some airlines employ ground staff to brief the pilots personally on important aspects of long haul flights they are about to undertake. The ground staff collate the relevant information so that the pilots get a clear picture in a relatively short space of time.

Aircraft preparation

While they were doing their flight planning in the crew room, the pilots will have agreed who is going to take the role of PF (pilot flying). Of course, the captain has the ultimate say in this matter. If the crew is flying more than one sector (take-off and landing) they will probably swap roles for subsequent sectors.

Having arrived at the aircraft PF will make his or her way to the flight deck to start preparing the aircraft for departure. Using a **checklist** he or she will ensure that all controls are correctly set and that all the aircraft flight manuals and emergency equipment are in place. The aircraft's **technical log** must be consulted to determine its maintenance status. (We'll look at the tech log in more detail later.) In the meantime PNF will be doing the **walkround** outside, examining the exterior condition of the airframe, engines, landing gear, probes and sensors. If there

Along with the airframe and engines, the landing gear must be inspected before every flight.

is any ice or snow accretion on the aircraft during cold weather the ground servicing agent must remove it. De-icing is achieved by spraying hot de-icing fluid onto the affected surfaces using a high pressure hose mounted on a vehicle designed for this purpose. (Remember, it is not so much the mass of ice or snow, but rather its disruptive influence on the airflow round the aircraft which is critical.)

With PNF back in the flight deck the two pilots together will load the route into the flight management computer and then check that the route agrees with the ATC flight plan. The ground agent will present the pilots with a **load sheet**, giving the actual take-off mass of the aircraft and disposition of the payload. From this information the pilots will use the aircraft's take-off performance data to determine flap setting, engine power setting, stabilizer trim setting and V-speeds for take-off, each pilot checking the other's calculations to prevent errors.

The technical log

The aircraft's tech log is an important document having several sections. One deals with the **maintenance schedule**, which lays down how and when maintenance work must be carried out. The most basic check is the pre-flight walkround described above, which is carried out by PNF, and, in greater detail, by the ground engineer. More involved checks are scheduled periodically, either on specified dates or after the aircraft has flown a specified number of hours. From time to time the maintenance schedule calls for the aircraft to be virtually taken apart for close inspection and renewal of critical components.

With such a complex machine as a large modern airliner, it is perhaps not surprising to learn that it is highly unlikely that all its systems and equipment are in perfect working order all the time. When malfunctions occur that affect the airworthiness of the aircraft, they must clearly be rectified before it is allowed to fly again. But minor defects are often permitted to be deferred until rectification can be carried out at a more convenient time. Even here there are strict procedures which must be followed. If they are intending to accept for service an aircraft carrying **deferred defects** the pilots must consult the **minimum equipment list (MEL)**. The MEL will tell them firstly whether flight with a particular defect is permitted, and secondly whether any special procedures should be followed to compensate for the unserviceability. For example, if an engine driven generator is inoperative, the MEL will require the auxiliary power unit to be running throughout the flight with its generator taking the place of the inoperative one.

For every flight the aircraft makes, a fresh report page in the tech log must be completed. Each page includes a certificate stating how much fuel the aircraft departed with and this must be signed by the captain. If the aircraft was de-iced before departure this too is recorded. After flight the pilots must record the duration of the flight together with any new defects that have occurred and again the captain signs these entries.

Checklists

Checklists are a means of ensuring that the pilots operate the controls and systems in a predetermined manner and also that nothing has been omitted. Each phase of flight has its own checklist, which is a set of instructions or checks relevant to that phase. Typical phases are:

- flightdeck preparation
- before engine start
- after engine start
- before take-off
- after take-off
- approach
- landing

Time to go!

Let's put you in the flight deck left seat, the captain's seat. Scheduled departure time is approaching. All the pre-flight preparations are complete. You've checked the weather and notams, signed the tech log, and checked with your copilot the route and take-off performance calculations. Since you are PF for this sector, you have set the controls and systems yourself and briefed your copilot on take-off procedure, including the initial routing. You call for the before start checklist. The copilot reads each item and you give the appropriate response. If your response is incorrect the copilot will challenge it.

The ground personnel have connected the push back tug to your nosewheel with a long towbar. The senior cabin crew member confirms that the passenger count is correct and asks permission to close the door, which you grant. The copilot asks ATC for push back clearance and receives it. You advise the push back supervisor accordingly. He's standing under the nose, listening on his headset via a lead plugged into the aircraft. You hear him ask you to release the park brake, which you do. The tug pushes you back from the gate, the supervisor walking in attendance, until you are well clear, at which point the tug stops and you are asked to reset the brakes. The tug and bar pull away and the supervisor clears you to start your engines.

The engines are started one at a time, after which you dismiss the supervisor and call for the After Start checklist. Now the copilot gets taxi clearance from ATC. Out of the window you can see the supervisor giving you thumbs up, meaning all ground equipment clear. You wave acknowledgement and move the thrust levers forward, enough to get the aircraft moving, but mindful of the powerful blast behind the engines.

You ask the copilot to set the flaps for take-off and the senior cabin crew member comes into the flight deck to tell you that the cabin is secure for take-off, meaning that all galley equipment is stowed and all the passengers have their seat belts fastened.

ATC ground control hands you over to tower and you ask the copilot for the before take-off checklist. Tower clears you to line up. You confirm with the copilot that everything is ready and taxi onto the runway. Now tower clears you for take-off. You push the thrust levers forward and ... but you know the rest already!

757 being readied for service.

Framed by the propellers of a Hercules transport, this 747 is taxiing out for departure, wing tanks heavy with fuel.

113

12
Pilot Training

The physical ability to control an aircraft accurately on the ground and in the air is only one of the personal qualities demanded of the airline pilot. First and foremost he or she is a manager, responsible for the overall safe and efficient operation of the aircraft. And if things go wrong, rapid reaction time is no more important than the ability to think logically, make sensible decisions and if necessary review those decisions, continuing this process until the problem is solved.

Airline pilots will have their knowledge and skills tested regularly throughout their careers and copilots will be expected to achieve the same level of competence as captains because there is always the remote chance that the captain may become incapacitated during flight. During their years in the right hand seat copilots are serving an apprenticeship, building up experience for the day when they move over to the left seat. Under the captain's leadership the two pilots in a crew act as a team, monitoring each other's performance and consulting and communicating as required, the main difference between them being that the captain is the final arbiter and is the person responsible for the safe conduct of the flight in the eyes of the law.

How does someone get to be an airline pilot? All pilots, civilian and military, start their careers flying small, simple, single-engined propeller-driven aircraft. In these they learn the elements of aircraft handling. After a few lessons with an instructor there will arrive the momentous day when the student pilot is allowed to fly solo. Although this flight will invariably be restricted to one brief circuit of the airfield there is not a pilot in the world who has forgotten the thrill of his or her first solo.

The student pilot moves on to navigation, instrument flight and night flight. Initially navigation will be by map reading but gradually radio navigation techniques will be brought in. Eventually all the elements combine and the trainee will be able to fly at night, in cloud, without visual reference en route. There will also be plenty of ground subjects to study and take exams in.

Our future airline pilot must now learn to master bigger, faster, more complex twin-engined aircraft. At the end of his course he will be tested in his ability to fly these machines on instruments, navigating by radio beacons and maintaining communication with air traffic control while he does so. And he must be able to do all this and cope with simulated engine failure at any time. There will be no autopilot to ease the load.

The newly qualified pilot can now look for employment with the

first solo.

The student pilot moves on to navigation, instrument flight and night flight. Initially navigation will be by map reading but gradually radio navigation techniques will be brought in. Eventually all the elements combine and the trainee will be able to fly at night, in cloud, without visual reference en route. There will also be plenty of ground subjects to study and take exams in.

Our future airline pilot must now learn to master bigger, faster, more complex twin-engined aircraft. At the end of his course he will be tested in his ability to fly these machines on instruments, navigating by radio beacons and maintaining communication with air traffic control

Turning on to final approach. The realistic visual display belies the fact that this crew is in fact 'flying' a Boeing 757 simulator.

in ground school, learning the technical details and using the simulator 'on the ground' to practise systems operation in both normal and abnormal situations. Later on they will 'fly' the simulator, getting a feel for its handling characteristics and consolidating systems operation. The instructor will be able to expose the crew to situations that would be too hazardous to practise in a real aircraft, such as multiple systems-failures coupled with bad weather.

Aircraft training and line training

Having completed the simulator course, pilots go on to the real thing, practising take-offs, landings, rejected take-offs, simulated engine failures and go-arounds. The trainee captain or copilot will occupy his or her normal seat and a training captain will sit in the other. Needless to say, there will be no passengers aboard during this phase, which is called **aircraft training**.

The next phase is **line training**, which takes place on normal revenue flights, again with a training captain in the other seat. Having gained a satisfactory level of familiarity the new pilot will be assessed for proficiency by a different training captain. Successful completion of this **line check** confers authorisation on the new captain or copilot to act as both PF and PNF on normal revenue flights without the presence of a training captain.

The fidelity of the latest generation of simulators is high enough to permit aircraft training to be carried out in them, so-called 'zero flight time' training. Under this procedure, the first time a new pilot sits at the controls of the airliner he is being converted onto is at the start of his line training.

Periodic proficiency checks

All British airline pilots must be able to demonstrate proficiency in all areas of operation, including emergencies, up to the standards set by the Civil Aviation Authority, which is the regulatory authority in Britain. (Other nations have similar arrangements.) This test, the **proficiency check**, is carried out in the simulator with a training captain conducting the test and is repeated every six months. Pilots not meeting the required standard must be given further training. If they are still unable to pass the proficiency check they will lose their authorisation to operate revenue flights.

Once a year pilots must repeat the line check described above. This will be a normal revenue flight, with the captain and copilot under test occupying their normal seats. The training captain conducting the test will sit behind the crew to observe their performance.

Pilots must also undergo periodic training in matters such as operation of safety equipment and refresher training in other relevant subjects, such as new operating procedures.

Health checks

Captains are subjected to physical examination every six months, as are copilots over the age of forty. The examination is once a year for younger copilots. Corrective spectacles are allowed for pilots without perfect visual acuity. Indeed most of them will eventually need glasses for near vision as they get older.

Mounted on hydraulic jacks, the simulator can faithfully reproduce the motion sensation of aircraft in flight.

13
When it Goes Wrong

We have already made reference to the excellent safety record of the air transport industry. As long as safety takes overall precedence in the priorities of airline managements and regulatory authorities there is every reason to believe that the record can be further improved.

In the chapter on the rules of the air it was mentioned that the extensive regulation of the industry made a large contribution to safety standards. Of equal importance is the high level of technical standards demanded. Contrary to popular belief civil aviation does not lie at the cutting edge of new technology. The reason is obvious – it is not a good idea to install equipment in an airliner until its efficacy and reliability have already been proven in other applications. Even then, all the important systems in the aircraft will have back-up or alternate systems installed, as we saw when we looked at these systems earlier on.

Perhaps the most significant factor in flight safety is the proficiency of the personnel involved, both ground and air staff. For a person to be able to do his or her job well, he or she must be psychologically suited to it, motivated and trained. We have already looked at the personal qualities expected of airline pilots and we have seen that they must be able to demonstrate continuing proficiency by undergoing periodic checks.

Technical failures

As you would expect, the pilots will be familiar in some detail with the functioning of their aircraft's systems, but of course it would be impossible for them to know every last nut and bolt. For this reason the first action they take when technical problems occur is to consult the relevant checklist. We have already seen the importance of checklists during normal flight, the purpose of them being to make sure that the pilots operate the controls and systems in a predetermined manner and also that nothing is omitted. The same is true for abnormal situations. The procedure now is that PF will call for the relevant checklist and PNF will action it, with PF monitoring that the instructions are carried out correctly. If the problem is a serious one the captain may decide to take over the role of PF if up to then the copilot was in this role, at least until the problem is sorted out. Alternatively he may require the copilot to retain or take on the duties of PF in order to free himself of the task of physically controlling the aircraft and so give himself more mental capacity for dealing with the situation. Remember that the captain is the person legally responsible for the aircraft's safety.

Pilots practise dealing with abnormal situations when they are undergoing their proficiency checks in the simulator. Let's look at some examples.

Engine failure

Modern jet engines are incredibly reliable and failures extremely rare. Many pilots go through an entire career without experiencing one. But they must be prepared at all times, just in case. Earlier we looked at the case of engine failure during take-off and noted that the aircraft must be capable of either decelerating to a stop on the runway or else completing the take-off, depending on when the failure occurred. The rejected take-off procedure was also described. Once airborne, the aircraft must be able to continue to fly safely if an engine fails at any time.

If the engines are at high or moderate thrust settings when one of them fails the pilots will detect the malfunction straightaway from the effect on aircraft performance. The resulting thrust asymmetry will try to turn the aircraft in the direction of the failed engine and the loss of thrust will reduce the airspeed. On detecting an engine failure, then, the first priority for the pilots must be to ensure that the aircraft remains under control. Any tendency to turn must be prevented by rudder input. Excessive decay of airspeed can be prevented by … how would you do it? Either increased thrust on the functioning engine(s) or lowered pitch attitude (or both) will do the trick, depending on the intended flight path. If the autopilot is engaged but cannot cope it must be disengaged to allow manual control.

The next actions are to shut down the failed engine by closing its thrust lever and cutting off its fuel supply. Of course that engine will also have been powering other systems (electrical, hydraulic and pressurisation). The engine failure checklist which the pilots now carry out will make sure that the shutdown has been completed correctly and that the engine-driven systems are reconfigured as appropriate.

If the aircraft is at normal cruising flight level when the failure occurs it could be that even with the remaining engine(s) set to maximum thrust, the airspeed will decay below minimum acceptable. A lower pitch attitude will be needed to maintain minimum speed but of course this action will result in loss of altitude. If this is the case, clearance must be obtained from air traffic control to descend to a lower flight level.

The essentials dealt with, the pilots can now think about their subsequent course of action. If the aircraft is two-engined, it is important to minimise the time spent in the air with only one functioning engine remaining and so a diversion to the nearest suitable airport will be the next priority. This might well be the departure airport. The crew of a three- or four-engined aircraft will have the option of continuing the flight to a more convenient airport.

During the descent, with idle thrust set, engine failure is not so easy to detect. In fact the first clue the crew might have is malfunction of the systems the engine is powering. It will be necessary to check the engine instruments to get the full picture.

Suppose an engine was producing normal thrust but indicating other signs of ill health, such as low oil pressure. In this example, if the pilots allowed it to keep going it might eventually fail completely because of lack of lubrication. In cases such as this the engine shut-down checklist would be used to carry out a *precautionary* shutdown to prevent further damage.

Landing with an engine shut down is not a difficult manoeuvre. In a two-engined aircraft it is usual practice to fly the approach with a reduced flap setting, which reduces the thrust requirement on the remaining engine and ensures adequate climb performance if a go-around is required for any reason. Of course, the reduced flap setting demands a higher approach speed which in turn means that the runway distance required for landing will be greater.

Multiple engine failure

The chances of an airliner experiencing failure of more than one engine from mechanical causes are virtually zero. If multiple failures occur it is most likely to be due to other factors such as fuel starvation or ice build-up. Neither of these can occur if the crew are monitoring the fuel tank contents and using the aircraft's anti-icing system properly.

External factors might not be so easy to avoid, such as encountering volcanic dust clouds in the dark when they cannot be detected. (They will not show on weather radar because it relies on water drops to reflect its signals.) Known volcanic activity is promulgated in notams and pilots will give these areas a wide berth. If they do inadvertantly fly into volcanic dust there is a possibility that all the engines will malfunction. Most aircraft have checklist procedures for this situation which are designed to minimise the chances of complete failure and to restart engines if complete failure occurs.

When they are being tested prior to entering service, airliner engines have to demonstrate that they can withstand **birdstrikes**, in other words bird ingestion. Small birds frequently pass through the engines without the pilots even being aware of it. Larger birds can cause engine damage, but rarely enough to cause failure, although the captain might decide that a precautionary shutdown is necessary once the aircraft is at a safe height. In the worst case of an aircraft encountering a flock of birds just after getting airborne, it might be that more than one engine is affected but nevertheless it is virtually certain that there will be enough thrust to continue the take-off safely. Most major airports use bird scaring equipment to minimise this problem when flocks of birds are spotted close to the runway.

If the unthinkable happens and the aircraft suffers complete failure of all its engines, and none of them can be restarted, what then? Well, all is not lost. Remember that most airliners will glide at a descent gradient of about 1:20, with the force of gravity overcoming the aircraft's drag. From Flight Level 350 (35,000 feet on the standard altimeter setting) the gliding range is over 100 nautical miles. If there is an airport within gliding range an emergency landing can be made there. Otherwise the landing will have to be on the best surface the pilots can find (or on the sea). A difficult situation, but not impossible, and one that can be practised in the simulator, of course.

Pressurisation failure

If the cabin loses its air pressure oxygen is automatically provided for all passengers and crewmembers through individual masks. The pilots will start a rapid descent, reducing altitude to below 10,000 feet as soon as air traffic control and local terrain permit, whereupon normal breathing will be possible without the need for masks.

Fire

A fire occurring in one of the engines will ring a warning bell and bring on a warning light or caption in the flight deck. The pilots will immediately carry out the engine fire checklist, the essential items of which they will know from memory. This is the same as the engine failure checklist with the additional action of discharging the special extinguishers fitted for this purpose. These are controlled remotely from the flight deck.

Conventional extinguishers are used for dealing with any fires that may occur in the cabin. As an extra safeguard most aircraft toilets are nowadays fitted with smoke detectors.

Warning systems

We have already encountered two warning systems – the engine fire detection mentioned above and the stall warning system which shakes the control wheels if the aircraft's wings get too close to the stalling angle. System malfunctions are brought to the attention of the pilots either visually (by lights or captions) or aurally (beepers and horns) or both. Spoken aural warnings occur if the aircraft is approaching the ground too rapidly (sensed by the radio altimeters) or not in the landing configuration (flaps and landing gear down), or nearby aircraft are detected by the traffic alert and collision avoidance system.

The role of the cabin crew

Passengers usually see the cabin crew in the role of attending to their personal comfort during flight. Although this is their main task it is not the most important one. The cabin crew are there first and foremost as safety personnel. They are trained in the use of the on-board safety equipment, such as fire extinguishers, and also how to deal with medical problems. If a rapid evacuation of the passengers is necessary because of an emergency before take-off or after landing it is the cabin crew who will open the emergency exits, deploy the escape slides and supervise the evacuation procedure. As with the pilots, they undergo frequent testing of their knowledge and also refresher training when appropriate.

Human factors

Humans differ from machines in that they do not always perform their activities in a predictable manner. To a very large extent this short-coming can be overcome by training. In the operation of complex machinery such as airliners predictability is enhanced by the use of **standard operating procedures (SOPs)**. Pilots and cabin crew come in all shapes and sizes and with differing personalities. By following SOPs, efficient and safe operation of the aircraft can be guaranteed regardless of the personalities of the individual crew members.

Another human failing is physiological and psychological variability. Persons unsuited by nature to the roles of pilot or cabin crew are normally filtered out by selection procedures. But even those who are chosen will not perform perfectly every time they go to work. However, professionalism demands that they do their best even if they are tired or angry or depressed, and doing their best means meeting or exceeding the minimum standards set.

Passengers too have a contribution to make. For example, they can take the trouble to pay attention to the safety demonstration before take-off and to read the safety card – just in case. And by reciprocating the courtesy and consideration which the cabin crew extend to them they can help build a comfortable ambience in the cabin, to the benefit of all parties. Remember that the steward or stewardess who is serving you your meal may also be the one who helps to save your life in an emergency.

The trickiest human problem is that of crew fatigue, which can be defined as debilitating tiredness. A tired pilot will be able to perform his or her tasks properly, taking extra care to compensate for lack of fresh-ness. But the very ability to self-monitor is degraded by fatigue and herein lies the danger. In other words a fatigued pilot might not be aware that he or she is performing badly. There is a degree of protection in the presence of the other pilot in the crew, one of whose primary duties is to draw attention to errors made by his or her colleague. If both pilots in a crew are fatigued the implications for flight safety are obvious, particularly if their workload is compounded by factors such as technical problems or bad weather or making an approach into a difficult airport.

For this reason the regulatory authorities set maximum permitted durations of duty period for pilots. These maxima are governed by factors such as the time of day (or night) the duty commences and how many sectors (take-offs and landings) are to be carried out. The cabin crew must have similar protections because they too might have to carry out emergency duties at the end of the duty period. For very long flights, the rules demand the presence of an extra pilot in the crew to allow in-flight relief for the other two. Minimum lengths of rest periods between duties are also specified.

14
The Future

In the space of 100 years, air transport has evolved from flimsy wood-and-cloth contraptions barely able to carry their pilots aloft on the unreliable output of their puny engines to today's jet airliners, which can convey hundreds of passengers safely and swiftly many thousands of miles with a fuel efficiency better than that of motor cars.

As far as speed is concerned, further progress has been halted by a natural barrier – the speed of sound. Most of today's airliners cruise in the region of Mach number 0.8, which is of course 80% of this speed, and to improve the attractiveness of air travel the airlines instead turn to other areas such as passenger comfort, availability of amenities and fare price.

At the moment only one airliner type is capable of supersonic flight – the Anglo-French Concorde. The Concorde is a technical masterpiece, designed to transport its passengers at twice the speed of sound, albeit at fares beyond the pocket of the ordinary traveller. Environmentally, the Concorde's behaviour is not so good. Its fuel efficiency is well below that of the subsonics and the sonic booms which it generates as it cleaves the atmosphere prohibit it from overland supersonic cruising. During take-off and approaching to land the noise of its old-technology engines is an intrusion in a world where tranquillity is becoming ever more highly prized.

In terms of both time and money, the cost of development of a successor to the Concorde will demand the co-operation of aircraft manufacturers all over the world. If this hurdle can be overcome, and the problems of noise pollution and fuel profligacy resolved, it is probable that later generations of supersonic airliners will one day take to the skies to satisfy the demand for ever faster travel.

Subsonic aircraft of the future must also reduce their environmental impact. Fuel efficiency and noise suppression have improved substantially over recent decades, but nevertheless a Boeing 767 flying from Birmingham, England to Miami, Florida will typically consume some 45 to 50 tonnes of fuel, and every tonne of kerosene burnt generates three times this weight of carbon dioxide, the main culprit in trapping solar energy in the atmosphere.

Theoretically it is possible to design engines burning pure hydrogen, whose main combustion product is water vapour. But although not difficult to manufacture, cost of production of hydrogen is a major difficulty, as are storage and transportation. The fuel would have to be carried in liquid form, under pressure at very low temperatures. Fuel tanks would require heavy insulation to stop the hydrogen liquid warming up and boiling.

As a halfway house, methane would be a better fuel environmentally than kerosene because its ratio of carbon to hydrogen is the lowest of any hydrocarbon fuel. Compared to hydrogen, methane is relatively cheap to produce and relatively easy to store in liquid form. Naturally occurring methane is a greenhouse gas itself, so its consumption as a fuel (if collection is feasible) would substitute one pollutant for another, rather than adding to the total burden borne by the atmosphere.

Although subsonic cruising speed has reached its natural limit, navigational efficiency is still advancing. Computers in air traffic control centres and in airliners themselves allow more productive use of airspace as the density of traffic in the sky steadily grows. One likely development is greater direct control of flights from the ground, rather than by spoken radio communication between pilots and controllers as at present, with its attendant potential for misunderstandings, especially when communications are in English between participants for whom this language is not the mother tongue.

It is unlikely that complete control from the ground will ever be achieved, however, because there will always be occasions when problems can only be resolved with the judgement of a human mind on the flight deck, such as the necessity to deviate from the planned flight path in order to avoid hazardous weather or for technical reasons or to reconfigure aircraft technical systems after faults occur. Perhaps a system will evolve where a ground controller sends instructions directly to an aircraft's autopilot but the instruction will not be executed until the human pilots permit it.

Would one pilot alone on the flight deck be enough if air traffic control were 'flying' the aircraft? It is likely that one person could handle the workload during normal operations. But suppose the human pilot considers it necessary to intervene. Who will be there to assist him or her, and more importantly, to confirm or query his or her judgement and to monitor his or her actions? Perhaps as long as there are airliners in the sky there will always be a case for at least two humans on the flight deck.

Again, will our future pilots be able to fly their aircraft without the assistance of autopilots and computers when necessary if they never get the chance to practise these skills during normal operation? A related factor is that a pilot whose job is merely to watch the aircraft fly itself is unlikely to be as well motivated as one who can get his or her hands on the controls now and then. Designers of future aircraft and airline managers must address the issue of how much and under what conditions pilots should be allowed, or indeed encouraged, to fly manually and without guidance systems. It is likely that compared to a mere aircraft monitor, a skilled, motivated pilot will always make a greater overall contribution to flight safety.

Glossary

AI	attitude indicator	LVP	low visibility procedure
AOM	airport operating minima (weather)	m	metres
		Mach	ratio of TAS to speed of sound
APU	auxiliary power unit		
ASI	airspeed indicator	mb	millibars
ATC	air traffic control	MCP	mode control panel
ATIS	automatic terminal information service	MEL	minimum equipment list
		MFA	minimum flight altitude
°C	degrees Celsius	notam	notice to airmen
CB	circuit breaker (electrical)	PAPI	precision approach path indicator
CG	centre of gravity		
CTA	control area	PF	pilot flying
DA	decision altitude	PNF	pilot not flying
DH	decision height	QNH	sea level air pressure
DME	distance measuring equipment	RTO	rejected take-off
		RVR	runway visual range
FCC	flight control computer	SOP	standard operating procedure
FIR	flight information region		
FL	flight level	TAS	true airspeed
FMC	flight management computer	TCAS	traffic alert and collision-avoidance system
ft	feet	UHF	ultra high frequency
GA	go-around	V_1	maximum RTO speed
GPS	global positioning system	V_2	take-off safety speed
HF	high frequency	VFR	visual flight rules
HSI	horizontal situation indicator	VHF	very high frequency
		VNAV	vertical navigation
IAS	indicated airspeed	VOR	VHF omni radio (beacon)
IFR	instrument flight rules	VR	rotation speed (take-off)
ILS	instrument landing system	V_{ref}	reference landing speed
IRS	inertial reference system	VSI	vertical speed indicator
kg	kilograms	V-speeds	V_1, V_R and V_2
km	kilometres	ZFM	zero-fuel mass
LNAV	lateral navigation		

Index

Bold page numbers indicate main reference